P9-CEY-353

EYS 4.0

ENGAGE YOUR STRENGTHS

STRENGTHS AND SCRIPTURE ENGAGEMENT TO TRANSFORM YOUR WORLD

JOHN EDGAR CATERSON
CURT LIESVELD
ART PACE

American Bible Society
101 North Independence Mall East, FL8
Philadelphia, PA 19106

Gallup, Inc.
901 F Street, NW
Washington, D.C. 20004

Customization and design for *Engage Your Strengths 4.0* by Caleb Komorowski.
Edited by Stacey Wright and Davina McDonald.

The material in Section 1: Strengths Discovery is proprietary Gallup® and is used with permission.
Engage Your Strengths 4.0 authors: John Edgar Caterson, Curt Liesveld, and Art Pace.

Standard first edition 2009; EYS 2.0 edition 2012; EYS 4.0 edition 2014

ABS Item #124423 – ABS *Engage Your Strengths 4.0*
ISBN #978-1-941449-96-7
ABS – 4/21-JD-5,000

10 9 8 7 6 5 4 3 2 1

For my bride Kristi –

You are the love of my life and my greatest source of strength.

You are the reason I want to look at the clouds.

–John Edgar Caterson

To my wife Rosanne –

Our marriage will always be my greatest success.

Your loving partnership continues to bring out the best of what God has put in me.

–Curt Liesveld

To my wife Mary –

Of all God's blessings in my life, you are the greatest.

"Grow old along with me! The best is yet to be."

–Art Pace

TABLE OF CONTENTS

FOREWORD

CHAPLAIN (MAJOR GENERAL) DOUGLAS L. CARVER,

(U.S. ARMY, RETIRED)

When I was the U.S. Army Chief of Chaplains, I first learned of American Bible Society's Armed Services Ministry and Gallup Faith Practice during a session break at the annual Strategic Leadership Development Training (SLDT) Conference on March 10, 2009. My Director of Sustainment and Information, Chaplain (Colonel) James Puchy, introduced me to Dr. John Edgar Caterson who represented both ministries. The meeting lasted less than a minute. However, it was enough to convince me that American Bible Society was serious about supporting the Army Chaplaincy in a collaborative effort to strengthen the religious needs of our chaplains, Soldiers, and their families.

My four years of ministry as the Army Chief of Chaplains came during a time when the United States was fighting dual wars in Iraq and Afghanistan. During my tenure, I was tasked with ensuring comprehensive and continuous religious support to a total of 1.2 million Soldiers deployed in more than eighty nations, 300,000 Department of Defense civilians, and 700,000 military families. Additionally, I was responsible for the professional development and pastoral care of 2,900 Chaplains and Chaplain Assistants in the active Army, the Army Reserves, and the Army National Guard whose primary responsibility focuses on facilitating the religious needs of the Army. It was a calling that I did not take lightly and I welcomed those faith-based organizations like American Bible Society who were willing to partner in equipping and sustaining the religious support mission of our Unit Ministry Teams (Chaplains and Chaplain Assistants).

My second encounter with the Armed Services Ministry and Gallup

Faith Practice was in my office at the Pentagon on April 30, 2009. I later learned that representatives of these two ministries had previously met in Washington, DC to prayerfully consider how to help me accomplish the Army Chaplaincy strategic ministry vision. In short, my vision was to provide our Chaplains with the appropriate training, resources, and pastoral care in their support of an Army at war, and to shape the future culture of the Chaplain Corps. During this particular office call, an important statement was made regarding why our military families were so crucial to the future of the Nation:

"We're not simply concerned about the religious needs of the two million that have deployed to Southwest Asia since the attacks on September 11, nor the twenty-four million men and women comprising the current Veteran population. We must also look for ways to reach out to the fathers and mothers, sons and daughters, brothers and sisters, grandparents, aunts and uncles of active duty, and retired military members. This comprises more than 100 million people – that is a third of our nation . . . it is a significant people group, and mission field, who needs to have access to the absolutely best scriptural resources!"

During our meeting Dr. Caterson made a proposal about the *Engage Your Strengths* program. He said, "What if the power of God's Word and the personal strengths of Chaplains and Soldiers were unleashed to become living and active throughout the military?" He went on to say, "This resource/program will be designed to assist leaders and military Chaplains of all ranks, encouraging them in their service to the Nation and, ultimately, strengthening the spiritual resilience of our Soldiers and their families."

As our meeting concluded, we agreed that the first step would be to work with the Chaplain faculty and staff at the United States Army Chaplain

Center and School to test the program with their Chaplain students as well as a number of our major Army Commands. Over the course of the following two months the program was introduced to senior Chaplains at the U.S. Army Medical Command; U.S. Army Installation Management Command; U.S. Army Training and Doctrine Command; U.S. Central Command; U.S. Special Operations Command; and the United States Military Academy. It was also presented to Chaplains serving in several critical Army-wide programs, including the U.S. Army Family Life Chaplain and Resource Centers; Family and Morale, Welfare and Recreation Directorates; the U.S. Army Chaplaincy Religious Education Program; the Comprehensive Soldier Fitness program; and Soldier and Family Ministries.

On July 1, 2009 my staff provided an update on the *Engage Your Strengths* resource. They further recommended that I approve the continued program development of this cutting edge religious education tool, including a formal presentation of EYS to the senior Unit Ministry Teams at the annual Army Chaplain Corps' Senior Leader Development Training (SLDT) in February 2010.

Chaplain (Colonel) Ken Bush, Director of Training at the U.S. Army Chaplain Center and School, sent a memorandum to all the senior Army Chaplains and Chaplain Assistants attending SLDT 2010, outlining *Engage Your Strengths*:

> ***Engage Your Strengths*:** During registration you will receive [an] exciting new ministry enhancing tool . . . *Engage Your Strengths*. It blends Gallup's popular StrengthsFinder® assessment and coaching process with biblical foundations and extended Scripture engagement. *Engage Your Strengths* builds on the belief that everyone has God-given talents that become strengths when coupled with skills and knowledge.

> As men and women refine and practice their strengths they will be equipped to consistently achieve excellence and maximize their God-given talents. The goal is to build personal resilience in Soldiers and Families by enabling them to live their strengths and engage God's Word daily. In the long run this will shape the culture and help keep Army communities strong.

The following year Chaplain Bush sent a second memorandum to senior Army Chaplain Corps leaders attending the 2011 Army Chaplaincy Senior Leader Development Training:

> ***Engage Your Strengths*:** During last year's Strategic Leader Development Training and CAST events we gave every Chaplain, Chaplain Assistant, and Director of Religious Education in attendance a copy of *Engage Your Strengths*. Many of you took the time to experience the value of this assessment first-hand and some of your Unit Ministry Teams have successfully used the material in a wide range of venues. I encourage you to use the enclosed revised *Engage Your Strengths* Quick Start Guide to walk through the process . . . I believe that you will find the insights very helpful for your own leadership development and discover a tool with a wide range of applications in your ministry. As a part of this initiative we trained a number of coaches across the Corps who can serve as a resource for you to further explore your strengths and their significance. The ladies of the Protestant Women of the Chapel (PWOC) have adopted this material with their own unique design and have trained *Engage Your Strengths* coaches who are available on many of your installations.

For four straight years, U.S. Army Chaplains (along with Air Force, Navy, Marine, & Coast Guard Chaplains) were trained with *Engage Your Strengths*. My good friend, Dr. John Edgar Caterson, and Reverend Curt Liesveld,

Gallup® Strengths Coach and Consultant, made countless trips to the United States Army Chaplain Center and School and the Armed Forces Chaplaincy Center (AFCC) to facilitate this valuable training resource.

I was inspired by their passion. It seemed that everywhere I traveled to visit our Unit Ministry Teams and Soldiers – whether in United States Forces-Europe, U.S. Pacific Command, or the myriad of camps, posts, or stations in the continental United States, they were there training Chaplains, leaders, and family members to engage and live out their God-given strengths.

Shortly before retiring as the Army Chief of Chaplains, I had an opportunity to address American Bible Society's Board of Trustees. During my remarks I made the statement, "What makes *Engage Your Strengths* unique is its deep dive into Scriptures that illuminate a Chaplain's spiritual giftings and foster daily Scripture engagement. *Engage Your Strengths* is a game-changer. It has the potential to transform the culture of the military chaplaincy, the Army, the extended Army family, and the entire Nation."

After retiring from the Army in 2011, I accepted a new ministry assignment as the Executive Director of Chaplaincy Services for the North American Mission Board (NAMB) of the Southern Baptist Convention. One of my pressing goals in this pastoral position is to use my experience with *Engage Your Strengths* to increase the collaborative ministry effort between our Chaplains, military community, and local churches. Chaplains have a wealth of ministry experience, professional education, and pastoral leadership that can greatly assist the local church in its ministry to the surrounding community.

In 2012 American Bible Society released *Engage Your Strengths 2.0, Military and Church Edition*. It has been a tremendous help to bridge the gap between the church and military, and between pastors and Chaplains.

Engage Your Strengths continues to fuel strengths discovery, strength coaching, strengths-based leadership for teams, and encourage deeper engagement with the Holy Bible. Since its initial rollout, over 40,000 have benefitted from this revolutionary program.

I was thrilled to recently learn that Chaplain (Colonel) Art Pace (U.S. Army, Retired) was named as the Executive Director of Armed Services Ministry. Art was one of the Army Chaplaincy's most devoted and humble men of God. With a sincere and compassionate heart, he equipped our Soldiers and families to live out their faith while serving in uniform. I'm excited that he has collaborated with both John Edgar and Curt on the *Engage Your Strengths 4.0* resource. I believe, with this dynamic team in place, the EYS program will impact tens of thousands, if not generations, of men and women affiliated with the Armed Forces community.

Douglas L. Carver

Chaplain (Major General)
United States Army, Retired
Executive Director of Chaplain Services
North American Mission Board (NAMB)

PREFACE
TO THE FOURTH EDITION

As you read this book, you will find that much of the text in sections 1 and 2 are the same as found in the earlier editions of *Engage Your Strengths*. The content in Section 1 is Gallup® proprietary material and we are grateful to Gallup® Faith Practice for allowing us to utilize it once again for this edition. You will notice a very significant improvement to *Engage Your Strengths 4.0:* stories. In preparation for this edition, we asked a number of our 'EYS Champions' to provide their stories – especially as they live out their strengths and interact with the Scriptures. We have also included a number of key tools in Section 3 – Coaching Tools. First, we asked a number of our 'EYS Coaches' to provide coaching stories of individuals and of churches. We have been inspired by their stories and trust you will be as well. Second, we have provided coaching exercises. Lastly, there is the Theme Insight Card content with the bonus of the theme Balconies and Basements content.

We trust that this *Engage Your Strengths 4.0* edition will impact your life and expand your ministry. We hope that it gives you a greater appreciation for the fact that you are fearfully and wonderfully made, and to accept your natural, God-given talents is to accept yourself the way God created you. May this empower you to engage your strengths daily and live out the Word of God more fully as you transform your world.

Blessings,

Dr. John Edgar Caterson, D. Min.

Rev. Curt Liesveld, M. Div., M.A.

Chaplain (Colonel) Art Pace (U.S. Army, Retired), M. Div., M.A.

INTRODUCTION

There are some natural questions that arise when we seek to live our lives for Christ. Why do we make the choices we do? Why do some things come naturally, while others don't? Why are we drawn to certain activities and not to others? There's a simple, but powerful reason: our God-given talents. When we understand our unique talents, we have the potential to harness them; our whole world can change.

There is something within our spirit that resonates with the discovery of our talents and strengths. It "feels right," as though from the depths of our being we can finally shout, "This is who I was created to be!" This liberating experience allows us to develop and move toward, living out our talents — God-given ways of thinking, feeling, or behaving. It also gives us permission to accept ourselves as God originally created us to be.

We see talent in people around us every day. We can observe the patterns of thought, feeling or behavior that give them a unique edge. Sometimes, it may even seem effortless. In fact, our talents are the keys to our innate potential. When we tap into them we act with more confidence, inspiration and direction.

Imagine if the power of God's Word and your strengths were unleashed to become living and active throughout the world. What if you could move toward the extraordinary and live every day in this reality of being fearfully and wonderfully made? Would you do it? Would you be willing to invest the time and energy necessary to discover the God-given potential that already resides within you and is waiting to be unleashed?

From a spiritual viewpoint, when we affirm and engage our strengths in

Scripture, we communicate to God our gratefulness for gracing us with our unique mix of talents and gifts, and learn to live the life that God always intended us to live. It also gives us a sense of significance and purpose, and a new set of lenses with which to encounter the life-changing message of the Word of God!

Like everyone, we are at our best when we do what God created us to do. Our talents are an important key. They were placed into us by our Creator, and we must draw them out.

In the following pages you will experience an amazing adventure. Section 1 is on "Strengths Discovery" and will take you through the process of learning about strengths, unpacking you greatest talents, and moving towards Strengths-based leadership. Section 2, on "Strengths and Scripture Engagement," will provide you with a couple of recommended reading plans for getting the most out of God's Word, Scripture engagement, the 34 talent deeper dives, and EYS stories. Finally, Section 3, "*Engage Your Strengths* for Life," will feature content from the Gallup® Theme Insight Cards, helpful content on talent Balconies and Basements, and stories from EYS coaches.

Before you dive in, start your journey by taking Gallup®'s Clifton StrengthsFinder® assessment. You will find instructions on how to take the Clifton StrengthsFinder® on page 33. Then get ready to embark on an adventure that will transform your Christian life and maybe even your world.

For the body itself is not made up of only one part, but of many parts. If the foot were to say, "Because I am not a hand, I don't belong to the body," that would not keep it from being a part of the body. And if the ear were to say, "Because I am not an eye, I don't belong to the body," that would not keep it from being a part of the body. If the whole body were just an eye, how could it hear? And if it were only an ear, how could it smell? As it is, however, God put every different part in the body just as he wanted it to be. There would not be a body if it were all only one part! As it is, there are many parts but one body.

–1 Corinthians 12.14-20

SECTION 1
Strengths Discovery

Make a careful exploration of who you are and the work you have been given, and then sink yourself into that. Don't be impressed with yourself. Don't compare yourself with others. Each of you must take responsibility for doing the creative best you can with your own life.

Galatians 6.4-5 *(The Message)*

Chapter 1

THAT'S IMPRESSIVE. THAT'S A STRENGTH.

Emily did it with ease. The funny thing is, she can do it practically anytime she wants.

Everyone in the workgroup is stressed and tired. The project is daunting and the deadline is looming. The day has been long, and everyone knows it's going to get longer. Morale is waning — but Emily is going to do something about it.

Fifteen minutes later, the office is humming. Emily's associates, the same people who were mentally exhausted and nearly defeated just a short time ago, are re-energized, confident, and focused on meeting the challenge at hand.

Some in the group are smiling at each other. They know what just happened. They've seen it before: Emily has an uncanny ability to "rally the troops." No one else in the group could have done it, but Emily did it with ease.

The funny thing is, she can do it practically anytime she wants.

That's impressive.
That's a strength.

Gallup® has extensively studied the nature of strengths, and has discovered the answers to questions that had to be asked: What is the secret behind strengths? Can everyone have strengths? How are strengths created?

In *Engage Your Strengths* you'll find the answers to those questions and many more. In brief but substantial sections, you'll not only learn about strengths; you'll also take active steps toward making the most of your innate potential for excellence.

Start With What's Right

> *The field of psychology was based almost entirely on the study of what is* ***wrong*** *with people.*

In the early 1950s, Donald O. Clifton, who would go on to be named the "Father of Strengths Psychology," noticed a major problem: The field of psychology was based almost entirely on the study of what is wrong with people. He wondered if it would be more important to study what is right with people.

So, over the next five decades, Don and his colleagues at Gallup took a very close look at the **talents** of highly successful people, focusing on the positive instead of the negative. Millions of in-depth interviews were conducted to determine the most natural thoughts, feelings, and behaviors of "the best of the best."

They quickly discovered that our talents do more than make us unique individuals. Our greatest talents — the ways in which we most naturally think, feel, and behave — also serve as our best opportunities for excellence when they are followed.

> *Sure, skills are important. And knowledge is vital. But strength requires something more important and powerful than skill and knowledge combined.*

Start With Talent

Maybe you've heard someone describe a great basketball player by saying, "He has skills."

And perhaps you've heard a world-class computer programmer described with the compliment "She really knows what she's doing."

Well, both of those comments would be true. Any basketball player has **skills**. Any programmer has **knowledge**. But greatness requires more than skill and more than knowledge. In fact, strength — the greatness that consistently delivers a positive outcome through near-perfect performance — requires something more important and powerful than skill and knowledge combined:

Strength requires talent.

Sure, skills are crucial. Without skill — the basic ability to move through the fundamental steps of a task — a basketball player wouldn't be able to go through the essential motions of shooting a basket.

And knowledge is vital. A computer programmer couldn't even begin without knowledge of the general rules of programming.

But with training and education, pretty much anyone can go through those fundamental steps or possess that basic knowledge. Great basketball players, average basketball players, and even bad basketball players go through the same fundamental motions while shooting the ball. And whether they are good, average, or bad, all computer programmers have knowledge of the general rules of programming.

The very best, however, have a big edge. They have discovered the power of following their unique natures. They recognize the tremendous potential of building upon their greatest talents — the ways in which they most naturally think, feel, and behave.

The best of the best know that to finish with strength, you must start with talent.

- **Knowledge** *(nälij) n. what you know*
- **Skill** (skĭl) n. *the basic ability to move through the fundamental steps of a task*
- **Talent** (tal′ənt) n. *a natural way of thinking, feeling, or behaving*

Is "Zillion" A Real Number?

Sure, we all recognize that "everyone is different" and that we're all "special" and "unique," but all too often we give only surface attention to this deeply important insight.

> ***No. "Zillion" is not a real number — but it is a word you might be tempted to use if you tried to list all of the talents found among humankind.***

It's not until you take a really close look at talents and begin to discover the amazing variety and intricacy of how we each naturally think, feel, and behave that you start to understand just how truly unique we each are. You'd also realize that creating a comprehensive list of human talents is pretty much an impossible task.

But our talents represent our natural power and potential -— our greatest opportunities for personal and career success — so we need a way to at least begin thinking and talking about them.

That's where **themes** are a big help.

> *Themes are a starting point for thinking and talking about talents.*

Maybe you can't list each and every talent, but if you take a step back, you will see that talents often have something in common: a theme that connects them.

Some talents — like natural tendencies to share thoughts, to create engaging stories, and to find the perfect word — are directly connected to communication. That's what they have in common — their theme — so to begin thinking and talking about them, we can call them Communication talents.

Other talents — such as natural dependability, sense of commitment, and avoidance of excuses — have a responsibility theme, so we identify them as Responsibility talents.

> *Competition*
> *Discipline*
> *Empathy*
> *Intellection*
> *Positivity*

We don't have a list of each and every talent, but we do have the next best thing: themes that connect them and give us a great starting place for discovering our talents and for learning even more about our potential for strength.

- **Theme** *(thēm) n. a category of talents*

Themes Are The Basic Language Of Talent

> *Decades of research into talents and success have shown that the talents most directly related to potential for success can be grouped into 34 themes.*

Achiever

People especially talented in the Achiever theme have a great deal of stamina and work hard. They take great satisfaction from being busy and productive.

Activator

People especially talented in the Activator theme can make things happen by turning thoughts into action. They are often impatient.

Adaptability

People especially talented in the Adaptability theme prefer to "go with the flow." They tend to be "now" people who take things as they come and discover the future one day at a time.

Analytical

People especially talented in the Analytical theme search for reasons and causes. They have the ability to think about all the factors that might affect a situation.

Arranger

People especially talented in the Arranger theme can organize, but they also have a flexibility that complements this ability. They like to figure out how all of the pieces and resources can be arranged for maximum productivity.

Belief

People especially talented in the Belief theme have certain core values that are unchanging. Out of these values emerges a defined purpose for their life.

Command

People especially talented in the Command theme have presence. They can take control of a situation and make decisions.

Communication

People especially talented in the Communication theme generally find it easy to put their thoughts into words. They are good conversationalists and presenters.

Competition

People especially talented in the Competition theme measure their progress against the performance of others. They strive to win first place and revel in contests.

Connectedness

People especially talented in the Connectedness theme have faith in the links between all things. They believe there are few coincidences and that almost every event has a reason.

Consistency

People especially talented in the Consistency theme are keenly aware of the need to treat people the same. They try to treat everyone in the world with consistency by setting up clear rules and adhering to them.

Context

People especially talented in the Context theme enjoy thinking about the past. They understand the present by researching its history.

Deliberative

People especially talented in the Deliberative theme are best described by the serious care they take in making decisions or choices. They anticipate the obstacles.

Developer

People especially talented in the Developer theme recognize and cultivate the potential in others. They spot the signs of each small improvement and derive satisfaction from these improvements.

Discipline

People especially talented in the Discipline theme enjoy routine and structure. Their world is best described by the order they create.

Empathy

People especially talented in the Empathy theme can sense the feelings of other people by imagining themselves in others' lives or others' situations.

Focus

People especially talented in the Focus theme can take a direction, follow through, and make the corrections necessary to stay on track. They prioritize, then act.

Futuristic

People especially talented in the Futuristic theme are inspired by the future and what could be. They inspire others with their visions of the future.

Harmony

People especially talented in the Harmony theme look for consensus. They don't enjoy conflict; rather, they seek areas of agreement.

Ideation

People especially talented in the Ideation theme are fascinated by ideas. They are able to find connections between seemingly disparate phenomena.

Includer

People especially talented in the Includer theme are accepting of others. They show awareness of those who feel left out, and make an effort to include them.

Individualization

People especially talented in the Individualization theme are intrigued with the unique qualities of each person. They have a gift for figuring out how people who are different can work together productively.

Input

People especially talented in the Input theme have a craving to know more. Often they like to collect and archive all kinds of information.

Intellection

People especially talented in the Intellection theme are characterized by their intellectual activity. They are introspective and appreciate intellectual discussions.

Learner

People especially talented in the Learner theme have a great desire to learn and want to continuously improve. In particular, the process of learning, rather than the outcome, excites them.

Maximizer

People especially talented in the Maximizer theme focus on strengths as a way to stimulate personal and group excellence. They seek to transform something strong into something superb.

Positivity

People especially talented in the Positivity theme have an enthusiasm that is contagious. They are upbeat and can get others excited about what they are going to do.

Relator

People especially talented in the Relator theme enjoy close relationships with others. They find deep satisfaction in working hard with friends to achieve a goal.

Responsibility

People especially talented in the Responsibility theme take psychological ownership of what they say they will do. They are committed to stable values such as honesty and loyalty.

Restorative

People especially talented in the Restorative theme are adept at dealing with problems. They are good at figuring out what is wrong and resolving it.

Self-Assurance

People especially talented in the Self-Assurance theme feel confident in their ability to manage their own lives. They possess an inner compass that gives them confidence that their decisions are right.

Significance

People especially talented in the Significance theme want to be very important in the eyes of others. They are independent and want to be recognized.

Strategic

People especially talented in the Strategic theme create alternative ways to proceed. Faced with any given scenario, they can quickly spot the relevant patterns and issues.

Woo

People especially talented in the Woo theme love the challenge of meeting new people and winning them over. They derive satisfaction from breaking the ice and making a connection with another person.

Activity

Consider these talents (below) and themes (on the right). For each group of talents, identify the theme that connects them.

A natural anticipation of the needs of others, an instinctual sense of another person's emotions, and ease in seeing the world through the eyes of others

are ____ talents.

An inherent desire to win, natural attraction to contests, and an instinctual need to compare performances

are ____ talents.

An easy smile, a natural generosity with praise, and a consistently energetic and optimistic outlook

are ____ talents.

A knack for order and structure, an inherent desire for precision, and a natural appreciation of timelines and deadlines

are ____ talents.

A tendency to muse and reflect, an enjoyment of mental exercise, and naturally thoughtful introspection

are ____ talents.

How did they do that? The Answer *is* simple: It *is* easy for him. She is a natural.

You've seen strength in action — and when you did, the excellence it delivered probably stood out. When you were fortunate enough to be on the receiving end of a strength, you might have appreciated it greatly — and perhaps even thought "He made that look so easy" or "She's a natural!"

> *Discover your greatest talents, and you'll discover your greatest opportunity for strength.*

And when the performance was particularly impressive, for a moment you might have wondered, "How did he *do* that?"

That's an excellent question, and though the answer might not be obvious, it is simple:

It *is* easy for him. She *is* a natural.

Each is performing at such a high level simply by building upon how he or she most naturally thinks, feels, and behaves: their greatest talents.

Of course, any level of talent can be helpful. If you're a customer service representative for whom a friendly manner, anticipation of the needs of others, and rapid problem-solving are lesser talents, you'll be able to perform that role — but not very well. Why? Because some of the most important talents required for the role simply don't come to you very naturally.

What if a friendly manner, anticipation of the needs of others, and rapid problem-solving come to you more naturally? If those are among your *supporting* talents, you certainly would be a better customer service repre-

Answers: 1. Empathy 2. Competition 3. Positivity 4. Discipline 5. Intellection

sentative. In fact, you might be pretty competent, although relying on your supporting talents through a full day of work could be awkward and draining.

But if a friendly manner, anticipation of the needs of others, and rapid problem-solving are some of your *dominant* talents, you'd really be in your element as a customer service representative. You'd rapidly pick up the skills and knowledge required for the role. You'd instantly become friends with the customers. You'd know their needs almost before they begin speaking, and you'd practically have the problem solved before they finish.

You would be performing with strength.

You would be consistently delivering a positive outcome through near-perfect performance.

You would be the person about whom everyone is asking, "How does he *do* that?"

Discover your greatest talents, and you'll discover your greatest opportunity for strength.

We all need help in discovering our greatest talents.

So what *are* your greatest talents?

That question can be easy to answer, yet difficult at the same time.

> *That's where the Clifton StrengthsFinder® comes in.*

Your greatest talents are hiding in plain sight. The ways in which you most naturally think, feel, and behave as a unique individual are such a dominant part of you that they are always there — everywhere you go, and in everything you do.

But because your greatest talents are such a natural part of you, they might be harder for you to find than they are for anyone else. You experience them all day, every day. To you, your greatest talents might seem commonplace. To you, they might even be invisible. Even your closest family members and friends, and the people with whom you work every day, might not easily recognize your greatest assets and the tremendous power and potential they hold.

Again, though, your greatest talents are in plain sight. And they leave clues everywhere. But the clues need to be found, and they need to be put together in a way that makes sense — and that could take a very long time.

We all need a little help in discovering our greatest talents.

That's where the Clifton StrengthsFinder® comes in.

The Clifton StrengthsFinder® will put you on the path to discovering your greatest talents.

Grounded in more than five decades of the study of talents, strengths, and success, the Clifton StrengthsFinder® was released to the public in 1998. Since that time, more than 11 million people have used this online instrument as a starting point in discovering their greatest talents.

Now it's your turn.

The Clifton StrengthsFinder® is an invaluable tool as you seek the source of your natural power. By gathering your instantaneous reactions to 180 sets of paired statements, it pulls together important clues to the ways in which you most naturally think, feel and behave as a unique individual.

Using your reactions to those statements, the Clifton StrengthsFinder® measures your talents in 34 categories called themes. It then ranks those themes by how dominant your talents in them appear to be, as indicated by your responses.

Finally, the Clifton StrengthsFinder® gives you a report of your Signature Themes — a ranked listing of the five themes that seem to hold your most dominant talents.

To take the assessment, you'll need to purchase a Registration Key from the Gallup® Strength Center. It's a unique identifier that will allow you one Clifton StrengthsFinder® assessment. Further instructions are on page 33 of this book.

After a few demographic questions, your assessment will begin. (Make a note of your username and password, as you'll need them each time you want to log back into your account.)

Be sure to reserve at least 45 minutes during which you can focus solely on your assessment. Because the Registration Key will allow you to take the Clifton StrengthsFinder® only once, and because you'll have only 20 seconds to respond to each pair of statements before the assessment moves on, you'll need to keep a consistent focus.

Of course, distractions can happen. If for some reason you're interrupted during your assessment and are unable to return within one minute, your responses will be saved and your assessment will be paused. When you return, your assessment will pick up at the point where you left it.

Immediately after completing your assessment, you'll receive a customized report of your Signature Themes. You'll have an opportunity to view and print two versions of your report: a certificate that displays your top five themes, and an expanded report that also offers descriptions of talents often found within those themes, along with some basic action items.

The remainder of this guide will assume that you have taken the Clifton StrengthsFinder® and that you have a copy of your Signature Themes and their full descriptions, so be certain to complete your assessment and print your full theme descriptions before beginning the next section.

- **The Clifton StrengthsFinder®** *(klĭf′tən strĕngths′fīndər) n. an online instrument that measures the presence of talents in 34 categories called "themes"*

STOP!

AND TAKE THE ASSESSMENT TEST BEFORE PROCEEDING WITH THIS STUDY

To take your assessment,
go to the following website and
purchase your code:
GallupStrengthsCenter.com

Chapter 2

YOUR GREATEST TALENTS

The Clifton StrengthsFinder® provides a tremendous group of clues to your greatest talents.

Welcome back!

> *What do you think of your Signature Themes?*

Now that you've taken the Clifton StrengthsFinder® assessment, you should have a customized report of your Signature Themes — a ranked listing of the five categories in which your most dominant talents probably can be found. It also provides general descriptions of the types of talents often found within those themes.

What do you think? How well do you feel your Signature Themes describe the ways in which you most naturally think, feel, and behave as a unique individual?

Many people are greatly pleased with their Signature Themes. They feel that the essence and value of who they naturally are have finally been put into words.

Others question their Signature Themes, feeling there's no way that a brief online assessment can peg who they are as unique individuals — and that neither they nor anyone else should be labeled.

Whichever of those two groups you fall into, you're right.

The Clifton StrengthsFinder® provides a tremendous group of clues to your greatest talents.

Does the Clifton StrengthsFinder® provide exciting insights about your talents? Absolutely. Does it put words to valuable characteristics that in the past felt indescribable and overlooked? You bet it does.

But does the Clifton StrengthsFinder® provide a complete, final-answer description of who you are? Absolutely not. And does it capture everything about you in five easy labels? That's impossible.

Using your own responses, the Clifton StrengthsFinder® provides a starting point — a tremendous group of clues to your greatest talents.

This is only the beginning. It's time to look for more clues, and your Signature Themes report has many to offer.

- **Signature Theme** *(sĭg'nəchər thēm) n. one of your top five categories of talents, as indicated by your responses to the Clifton StrengthsFinder®*

Activity

Your Signature Themes are a beginning, not an end.

Take a close look at the descriptions of talents associated with your top five themes — your Signature Themes. Because the Clifton StrengthsFinder® detects your greatest talents so well, it's likely that parts of the descriptions feel as if they were written specifically for you. But does each word fit you exactly? Probably not.

There's a good reason for that. The descriptions are based on research into the talents of millions of people, none of whose talents are exactly the same. Creating one description that would perfectly and thoroughly capture the talents of even two different people is simply not a reachable goal. So putting together a description that would exactly fit the talents of each individual in a worldwide audience was completely out of the question.

That's why the descriptions are somewhat general. They were created as a starting point, and customizing them to describe your unique talents is up to you.

To begin making your Signature Theme descriptions your own, grab a highlighter. Then carefully consider each description. Take your time. Think about each sentence, each phrase, and even each word.

Highlight the portions that best describe your dominant talents — the ways in which you naturally think, feel, and behave no matter where you are or what you are doing. Remember that your dominant talents are almost always active. Together, they provide a great description of who you most naturally are.

And if you feel your Signature Theme descriptions need more clarification to best reflect your greatest talents, make whatever additions you feel are appropriate. Make the descriptions feel comfortable to you.

Then you'll be ready to consider other clues to talent.

Your Clifton StrengthsFinder® Report: First Impressions

1. What was your first reaction to your Clifton StrengthsFinder® report?

2. What has your report helped you discover about your talents?

3. Did any part of your report surprise you?

4. Is there a particular theme you expected to see among your five Signature Themes, but it isn't there?

5. Have you shared your Clifton StrengthsFinder® report with anyone? What was that person's reaction?

List your Signature Themes.	**Describe a recent situation in which you applied talents from each theme.**
1.	
2.	
3.	
4.	
5.	

Your Clifton StrengthsFinder® Report: A Closer Look

Read the description of each of your five Signature Themes, and then highlight the parts that best describe you. Next, list your Signature Themes and describe a recent situation in which you applied talents from each theme.

Your Role and Your Signature Themes

We are most successful and most engaged when we use who we naturally are to fulfill the requirements of our roles. Most of us have many roles: spouse, parent, friend, employee, coworker, volunteer — the list can become quite long. What are some of your roles? What are the strengths required by these roles — the tasks you must consistently perform at a nearly perfect level?

Please list your five Signature Themes. Then list up to five strengths required of you on a frequent basis. Next, identify the theme or themes that help you excel in each of those tasks. Finally, answer the discovery questions on the next page.

Your Signature Themes

1.

2.

3.

4.

5.

Strengths: What tasks do your roles require you to consistently perform at a nearly perfect level?	Signature Themes: How will you leverage them?

Discovery Questions

1. Which of your Signature Themes seem most directly connected to the tasks required by your roles?

2. Which of your Signature Themes seem least connected to the tasks required by your roles?

3. Could you begin to more intentionally apply talents from any of your Signature Themes to those tasks? If so, what themes?

4. What overall strategies could you put in place to further capitalize on your Signature Themes in relation to your roles?

Exactly what is a strength?

> *Consistently near-perfect performance. That's strength.*

"**Strength**" sounds good, doesn't it? Think about the qualities associated with strength. Strength always delivers. Strength gets the job done, and does it right. You can count on strength.

Obviously, a strength is a good thing, regardless of whether it is one of your strengths or you are benefiting from the strengths of others. But exactly what is a strength? Well, in slightly more technical terms, a strength is the ability to consistently produce a nearly perfect positive outcome in a specific task.

Remember Emily? One of her strengths is her ability to motivate her coworkers when the going gets rough. She can consistently and nearly perfectly deliver the lift her teammates need in the most challenging times. Her associates know it, and they know they can count on that strength when it is needed.

Strengths are counted on, and they are appreciated. When you need a task done right, you look for strength. When you have received truly excellent service, you have benefited from a strength.

Consider these people who consistently deliver nearly perfect performance in a specific task:

- a call center representative who quickly "wins over" every upset customer
- a waiter who is consistently one step ahead of your needs

- a mom who always manages to meet the family's grocery needs on a limited budget
- a hotel clerk who always makes checking in an efficient, even pleasant experience
- a nurse who routinely administers injections so smoothly that patients "don't feel a thing"
- a school board president who consistently handles overloaded meeting agendas with great efficiency
- a retail associate who routinely creates displays that catch the eye of nearly every customer
- a bank teller who always recommends the perfect services for the customer's financial needs
- a salesperson who consistently builds long-term loyalty in client relationships

Strengths Always Deliver.

Activity

Take a moment to re-read the examples just given. Then consider how strengths are at work in your life.

Think about specific tasks that need to be performed at work, at home, and in other areas of your world. Then think about the people who perform those tasks with strength: you, your work associates, your family, and even people you might not know, but whom you encounter in your everyday life.

Finally, describe one strength that you see in yourself, and another that you see in someone else. Remember to be specific.

If you were describing a strength demonstrated by the nurse in one of our examples, it could look something like this:

The nurse at Dr. Jones' office **has the ability to consistently** *administer painless injections* **at a nearly perfect level.**

I have the ability to consistently ____________________

____

____

At a nearly perfect level.

____________________ **Has the ability to consistently**

____

____

At a nearly perfect level.

- **Strength** *(strĕngth) n. the ability to consistently produce a nearly perfect positive outcome in a specific task*

Activity

Talents, knowledge, and skills are the components of strength. You've learned the important differences between them; now prove your knowledge by correctly identifying each of these basketball-related resources as talent, knowledge, or skill. Circle the right answer.

1. **An innate desire** to outperform the competition

   Talent Knowledge Skill

2. **A grasp of the basic rules** of the game of basketball

   Talent Knowledge Skill

3. The ability to **perform the basic steps** of dribbling a basketball

   Talent Knowledge Skill

4. **Knowing the basic** plays your team runs during a game

   Talent Knowledge Skill

5. The ability to **perform the basic steps** of rebounding a basketball

   Talent Knowledge Skill

6. **A natural sense** of when opposing players are near

   Talent Knowledge Skill

Answers: 1. talent 2. knowledge 3. skill 4. knowledge 5. skill 6. talent

You're not only talented in areas; you're also talented in degrees°

Either you have it or you don't. Right? Wrong.

From a distance, a talent is a talent.

Self-discipline is self-discipline. That's it.

A positive outlook is a positive outlook. That's all.

The ability to produce ideas is the ability to produce ideas. End of story.

A talent is a talent. Either you have it or you don't. Right?

Wrong. That's ***not*** the way it is. When you take a closer look at your talents, you see that they exist in varying degrees.

Do you have any self-discipline? Sure you do — but how much?

Do you have at least some positivity? Yes — but how positive are you?

Do you sometimes have ideas? Of course you do — but how often?

You're not only talented in areas; you're also talented in degrees.

Some talents are so naturally powerful in you that they are dominant. No matter where you are or what you are doing, your **dominant talents** show up.

If the tendency to smile when you see another person is one of your dominant talents, you nearly always smile when you see another person. That talent is so natural in you that you practically can't turn it off. And in that smile — that talent — you have the power to light up the room.

You also have talents that can contribute, but don't come quite as naturally. Rather than dominate, your **supporting talents** show up only when their support is needed, and because they aren't as natural, they aren't as powerful.

Perhaps you can smile pretty easily when the situation calls for it, but it's not going to happen every time. And it's probably not going to be that light-up-the-room smile you'd get from someone in whom this talent is extremely natural. In you, this is a supporting talent.

And of course we all have our own **lesser talents** — ways of thinking, feeling, and behaving that don't come to us very naturally at all.

If the tendency to smile when you see another person is one of your lesser talents, it rarely shows up. And when it does appear, it might be forced. It's not that you're unhappy. You can smile when you see another person, but it's not likely to be a light-up-the-room smile, and you'd really rather not be in a situation where that's expected. Why? Because your most natural talents — your greatest power and potential — lie elsewhere.

Don't Stop with Your Signature Themes.

> *Your everyday life is filled with many other revealing clues to talent.*

Your Signature Themes provide tremendous clues to your greatest talents. The decades of science and millions of interviews behind the Clifton StrengthsFinder® allow it to bring language and a nearly tangible feel to the ways in which you most naturally think, feel, and behave. This is an excellent foundation to build on as you discover your talents.

But don't stop there. Your everyday life is filled with many other revealing clues to talent. Be sure to consider yearnings, rapid learning, flow, glimpses of excellence, satisfaction and barrier labels.

> *To what environments and activities are you naturally attracted?*

Yearnings can reveal the presence of a powerful talent, particularly when they are felt early in life. A yearning can be described as an internal force, an almost magnetic attraction, that leads you to a particular activity or environment time and again.

To what environments and activities are you naturally attracted? What natural ways of thinking, feeling, or behaving do they allow you to use?

Rapid Learning reveals other traces of talent. In the context of a new challenge or a new environment, something sparks your talents. Immediately your brain seems to light up as if a whole bank of switches were suddenly flicked to "on" — and the speed at which you anticipate the steps of an activity, acquire a new skill, or gain new knowledge provides a telltale clue to the talent's presence and power.

What activities do you seem to "pick up" quickly? What natural ways of thinking, feeling, or behaving do these activities allow you to use?

Flow happens when you become so engaged in an activity that you lose track of time. The activity may be new, but you instinctively know what comes next. It is also called Total Performance Excellence. It is the optimal state of intrinsic motivation. Simply ask yourself, "When are the times when all the pieces fell together?" "In what activities do you get 'lost in the moment?'" What are you doing when time seems to disappear?

Glimpses of Excellence are flashes of outstanding performance that have been observed by you or others. In these moments, the task at hand has tapped some of your greatest talents and directly displayed your potential for strength — consistent production of positive outcomes through near-perfect performance in that task.

In what activities have you or others glimpsed your potential for strength? What natural ways of thinking, feeling, or behaving do these activities allow you to use?

Satisfaction is psychological fulfillment that results when you take on and successfully meet challenges that engage your greatest talents. Pay close attention to the situations that seem to bring you these energizing experiences. If you can identify them, you will be well on your way to pinpointing some of your dominant talents.

What activities bring you the greatest satisfaction? What natural ways of thinking, feeling, or behaving do these activities allow you to use?

- To what environments and activities are you naturally attracted?
- What activities do you seem to "pick up" quickly?
- In what activities did you seem to automatically know the steps to be taken?
- What activities bring you the greatest satisfaction?
- In what activities have you or others glimpsed your potential for strength?

Chapter 3

TOWARDS STRENGTHS BASED LEADERSHIP

Barrier labels can be surprising clues to talent.

> *Great talents are often hidden BEHIND negative labels.*

Have you ever mistaken a powerful talent for a weakness?

Has anyone ever described your own greatest talents in belittling terms?

It happens. A weakness-seeking mindset or simple unfamiliarity can easily lead a person to misidentify and greatly undervalue exceptional talents.

Think about it: If you have dominant Activator talents, and you meet another person with the same dynamic drive to get things started, you probably will quickly recognize and appreciate those talents.

But what happens when your "Let's get going!" essence happens upon someone with highly Deliberative, "Let's think this through" talents? Because of your different natures, the encounter might be a bit frustrating. And because you are unfamiliar with each other's talents and their value, you might see them for what they aren't, rather than what they are.

The result? **Barrier labels**. One on you, and one on the other person.

Your dynamic Activator talents would be misidentified as careless impatience. Valuable Deliberative talents would be dismissed as overly cautious.

Talent would be disparaged, rather than celebrated. Potential strength would be stifled, instead of fulfilled. And a great partnership would never exist.

It doesn't have to be that way.

When you hear a barrier label, use it as a clue to talent.

When you are tempted to use a barrier label, don't do it. Instead, think about the value of the talents you might have overlooked.

Look for talents. You'll find them, and barrier labels can help.

Answers: 1. c 2. e 3. d 4. a 5. b

Activity

Match each barrier label (on the left) with the contribution that could be missed if the label is allowed to be a barrier, rather than used as a clue to talent.

With the proper discovery and development, . . .

1. A person labeled as bossy might
2. A person labeled as a pushover might
3. A person labeled as a workaholic might
4. A person labeled as unrealistic might
5. A person labeled as a chatterbox might

a. become an uplifting presence who finds the positive aspects of any situation
b. bring ideas to life by telling stories that are energizing and vivid
c. be a confident and powerful advocate on behalf of others
d. be an exceptional producer who inspires teammates by setting the performance bar high
e. invite the differing views of a variety of people and find valuable common ground

Is it a weakness? Maybe, maybe not.

> *Does it negatively affect your performance?*

We all have areas in which our talents, knowledge, and skills are greatest. So it just makes sense that we also have areas where the same assets aren't quite as abundant. Are those weaknesses? Maybe, maybe not.

If you're a behind-the-scenes automobile mechanic who never sees the customer and has little desire for contact with other people, is that lesser talent a weakness? No.

If you're a nurse who doesn't know how engines work, is that lack of knowledge a weakness? Not at all.

If you're a receptionist who struggles to perform the basic steps of administering an injection, is that shortage of skill a weakness? Of course not.

But what if you're an automobile mechanic who doesn't know how engines work, a nurse who struggles to perform the basic steps of administering an injection, or a receptionist who has little desire for contact with other people?

Now *those* are weaknesses.

The direct path to strength starts at your greatest talents. If you have a shortage of knowledge, skill, or talent that doesn't hurt your performance or that of others, it's not a big deal. It doesn't need your attention, and it certainly shouldn't detract from your efforts to build on how you most naturally think, feel, and behave.

But any lack or misapplication of knowledge, skill, or talent that *does* negatively affect your performance or that of others is a weakness — and because a weakness will prevent you or another person from performing with strength, it can't be ignored. It must be *managed.*

- **Weakness** *(wēk'nĭs) n. a lack or misapplication of knowledge, skill, or talent that negatively affects your performance or that of others*

If it's a weakness, MANAGE it.

When you have a weakness, something is missing. Somewhere in your knowledge, skill, or talents — or even in how you apply them — is a gap that prevents you from performing with strength.

> *Weaknesses in knowledge and skill can be managed with relative ease. A gap in talent is more of a challenge.*

To manage the weakness and create a strength, find the gap and fill it.

If it's a gap in knowledge, you can fill it through education. If it's a gap in skill, it can be filled through training. That's relatively easy.

Filling a gap in talent is more of a challenge.

> *Find the gap and fill it.*

Your talents are part of your nature, so you have to come by them naturally. You can't just run down to the corner store and buy a box of talents.

So what *can* you do? You can use intentional leverage, support systems, and complementary partnerships.

Intentional leverage is the conscious application of dominant or supporting talents that might not already be in play. A person with lesser talents in Empathy can intentionally call on his more powerful Individualization or Analytical talents to better understand how another person might be affected by a given situation.

A support system can be as simple as a calculator used by a person who has gaps in his mathematical talents. In a slightly more involved support system, a salesperson who has difficulty putting names with faces might create client portfolios that include not only the clients' names, but their photos as well.

A complementary partnership exists when two or more people help each other by sharing their talents, such as when a shy person invites an outgoing friend to parties to help break the ice, and when a naturally creative husband thinks of several fun vacation activities while the innately disciplined wife manages to fit them within the family's budget.

Think about your important tasks at work and at home. Are you performing them at the consistently productive and nearly perfect level of strength — or are there gaps you could fill?

Fill gaps in knowledge or skill with education and training. Manage gaps in talent through intentional leverage, support systems, and complementary partnerships. And be sure to apply your talents, knowledge, and skills *productively*.

When you find a gap, fill it. You'll take an important step toward performing with strength.

Learn the Language of Strengths.

> *By becoming familiar with these terms, you'll begin to maximize the power of your GREATEST talents.*

Barrier Label (băr′ēər lābəl)

n. a term used when talent is mistakenly devalued and dismissed as weakness. Unchecked, a barrier label can prevent talent discovery and strengths development – but when recognized it can be avoided and productively used as a clue to talent.

The Clifton StrengthsFinder® (klĭf′tən strĕngths′fīndər)

n. an online instrument that measures the presence of talents in 34 categories called "themes." The areas of talent measured by the CSF are those found to be most related to potential for success.

Dominant Talent (dŏm′ənənt tal′ənt)

n. a way of thinking, feeling, or behaving that naturally appears frequently and powerfully. No matter where you are or what you are doing, your dominant talents are active. Also referred to as your greatest talents, your dominant talents are your best opportunities for development of strengths.

Knowledge (nälij)

n. what you know. Knowledge can be acquired through formal or informal education.

Lesser Talent (lĕs′ər tal′ənt)

n. a way of thinking, feeling, or behaving that naturally appears rarely and with little power. Because they aren't very natural at all, lesser talents seldom contribute to strength.

Signature Theme (sĭg′nəchər thēm)

n. one of your top five categories of talents, as indicated by your responses to the Clifton StrengthsFinder®. Your Signature Themes are an excellent starting point as you seek to discover your most dominant talents.

Skill (skĭl)

n. the basic ability to move through the fundamental steps of a task. Skill can be acquired through formal or informal training.

Strength (strĕngth)

n. the ability to consistently produce a positive outcome through near-perfect performance in a specific task. To finish with strength, start with talent.

Supporting talent (səpôrt′ĭng tal′ənt)

n. a way of thinking, feeling, or behaving that naturally appears occasionally and with only relative power. Supporting talents surface only when their support is needed. Because they aren't as natural, supporting talents are unlikely to serve as a foundation for strength.

Talent (tal′ənt)

n. a natural way of thinking, feeling, or behaving. The more natural the talent, the greater its power, and the greater your opportunity for strength.

Theme (thēm)

n. a category of talents. Themes help you begin to discover and talk about your greatest talents. Decades of research into talents and success have shown that the talents most related to potential for success can be grouped into 34 themes.

Weakness (wēk′nĭs)

n. a lack or misapplication of knowledge, skill, or talent that negatively affects your performance or that of others. Because a weakness will prevent you or others from performing with strength, it must be managed.

Strengths-Based Leadership

"A leader needs to know his strengths as a carpenter knows his tools, or as a physician knows the instruments at her disposal. What great leaders have in common is that each truly knows his or her strengths — and can call on the right strength at the right time. This explains why there is no definitive list of characteristics that describes all leaders. It also explains why the calm and quiet approach of Mahatma Gandhi was equally as effective as the domineering and confrontational style of Winston Churchill."

— *D. Clifton*

The most effective leaders are always investing in strengths. In the workplace, when an organization's leadership fails to focus on individuals' strengths, the odds of an employee being engaged are a dismal 1 out of 11 (9%). But when an organization's leadership focuses on the strengths of its employees, the odds soar to almost 3 out of 4 (73%). When leaders focus on and invest in their employees' strengths, the odds of each person being engaged goes up eightfold.

The most effective leaders surround themselves with the right people and then maximize their team. While the best leaders are not well-rounded, the best teams are. Gallup's research found that top-performing teams have strengths in four specific domains.

The most effective leaders understand their followers' needs. People follow leaders for very specific reasons. When asked, followers were able to describe exactly what they need from a leader with remarkable clarity:

- **Trust**
- **Compassion**
- **Stability**
- **Hope**

4 Domains of Leadership Strengths

Executing	Influencing	Relationship Building	Strategic Thinking
• Achiever • Arranger • Belief • Consistency • Deliberative • Discipline • Focus • Responsibility • Restorative	• Activator • Command • Communication • Competition • Maximizer • Self-Assurance • Significance • WOO	• Adaptability • Developer • Connectedness • Empathy • Harmony • Includer • Individualization • Positivity • Relator	• Analytical • Context • Futuristic • Ideation • Input • Intellection • Learner • Strategic
Executing — Know how to make things happen; implement a solution; can "catch" an idea and make it a reality.	Influencing — Help team reach a much broader audience; sell team's ideas inside and outside organization; take charge and speak up for team; make sure team is heard.	Relationship Building — Essential glue that holds team together; can create a team and organization that are greater than the sum of its parts; synergistic.	Strategic Thinking — Keep team focused on what could be; absorbing and analyzing information; help team make better decisions; stretch team's thinking about the future.

SECTION 2

Strengths and Scripture Engagement

Since this is the kind of life we have chosen, the life of the Spirit, let us make sure that we do not just hold it as an idea in our heads or a sentiment in our hearts, but work out its implications in every detail of our lives. That means we will not compare ourselves with each other as if one of us were better and another worse.
We have far more interesting things to do with our lives.
Each of us is an original.

– Galatians 5.25-26 *(The Message)*

Chapter 4

GETTING THE MOST FROM GOD'S WORD

American Bible Society recommends two Bible reading methods designed to help you get the most from God's Word. Used by millions around the world, they are time-tested ways to engage Scripture as part of a life-long journey of growing intimacy with God.

The LORD says, "My word is like the snow and the rain that come down from the sky to water the earth. They make the crops grow and provide seed for planting and food to eat. So also will be the word that I speak — it will not fail to do what I plan for it; it will do everything I send it to do."

— Isaiah 55.1a, 10, 11

Suggested steps to help you dive deeper and live in your strengths:

1. Utilize one of two Bible reading methods as you work through your talents.

2. Read reflectively your top five signature talent themes (found on pages 67-198).

3. Begin to live out your God-given strengths, and share your discoveries with others you are journeying with, your small group, and your faith community.

THE PR3 METHOD
(PRAY, READ, REFLECT, RESPOND)

PRAY with focus and openness to see what God has for you. Pray for God's guidance and blessing.

READ the selected section of Scripture slowly and carefully. Take note of intriguing words and phrases. Read them a second time and meditate on what they are communicating to you.

REFLECT on what strikes you as you read. What does this passage of Scripture teach you about God's values?

How does the passage serve to deepen your understanding of God's Word and your relationship to God?

RESPOND to the passage. Speak to God directly about what's on your mind and in your heart. Open your mind and heart to what God's Word is communicating to you, and look for ways to live out what you've uncovered.

S for **Scripture**

Slowly and carefully read through the passage. Imagine what the people in the passage were experiencing. Write down a verse that stands out to you.

O for **Observation**

Write down your observations about the passage. Summarize the passage and think about what God has to say to you.

A for **Application**

Write down how the passage applies to your daily life.

How can you respond in the way Jesus taught?

P for **Prayer**

Write down an honest and heartfelt prayer. Remember that God always listens and already knows your needs.

The S.O.A.P. Method is used by permission of Life Resources - store.lifejournal.cc

Chapter 5

STRENGTHS LIVED OUT IN SCRIPTURE AND LIFE

Provided in this chapter is a closer look at 34 talents. Each talent contains its biblical underpinnings in the form of "Scriptural Support," "Primary Scripture Narrative," and "Deeper Dive" questions. To further explore, there is a Challenge and Appreciation for each talent as well as a story of how talent leads to strength lived out by an EYS Champion.

Achiever

Achiever Strength Highlight — *People strong in the Achiever theme have a great deal of stamina and work hard. They take great satisfaction from being busy and productive.*

Scriptural Support for the Achiever Strength

Proverbs 6.6-8 — Lazy people should learn a lesson from the way ants live. They have no leader, chief, or ruler, but they store up their food during the summer, getting ready for winter.

Hebrews 6.11,12 — Our great desire is that each of you keep up your eagerness to the end, so that the things you hope for will come true. We do not want you to become lazy, but to be like those who believe and are patient, and so receive what God has promised.

James 2.14-17 — My friends, what good is it for one of you to say that you have faith if your actions do not prove it? Can that faith save you? Suppose there are brothers or sisters who need clothes and don't have enough to eat. What good is there in your saying to them, "God bless you! Keep warm and eat well!" — if you don't give them the necessities of life? So it is with faith: if it is alone and includes no actions, then it is dead.

A Wife of Noble Character — Achiever at Work

Proverbs 31.1, 2, 8-31 — These are the solemn words which King Lemuel's mother said to him: "You are my own dear son, the answer to my prayers. What shall I tell you? . . . "Speak up for people who cannot speak for themselves. Protect the rights of all who are helpless. Speak for them and be a righteous judge. Protect the rights of the poor and needy." . . . How hard it is to find a capable wife! She is worth far more than jewels! Her husband puts his confidence in her, and he will never be poor. As long as she lives, she does him good and never harm. She keeps herself busy making wool and linen cloth. She brings home food from out-of-the-way places, as merchant ships do. She gets up before daylight to prepare food for her family and to tell her servant women what to do. She looks at land and buys it, and with money she has earned she plants a vineyard. She is a hard worker, strong and industrious. She knows the value of everything she makes, and works late into the night. She spins her own thread and weaves her own cloth. She is generous to the poor and needy. She doesn't worry when it snows, because her family has warm clothing. She makes bedspreads and wears clothes of fine purple linen. Her husband is well known, one of the leading citizens. She makes clothes and belts, and sells them to merchants. She is strong and respected and not afraid of the future. She speaks with a gentle wisdom. She is always busy and looks after her family's needs. Her children show their appreciation, and her husband praises her. He says, 'Many women are good wives, but you are the best of them all.' Charm is deceptive and beauty disappears, but a woman who honors the Lord should be praised. Give her credit for all she does. She deserves the respect of everyone."

Deeper Dive

- What motivated the Proverbs 31 Woman to be such a hard worker?
- What range of activity did she consider to be her field of work?
- What characterized the way in which she went about her business?
- How can you achieve your goals in ministry with similar Christ-like attitude?

Challenge: Use your stamina and hard work to accomplish Kingdom impact and lead by example.

Appreciation: Help an Achiever celebrate his/her accomplishments.

ENGAGE YOUR STRENGTHS STORIES

Dave Keller – *Chaplain, U.S. Army Reserves*

As a former Army Infantry Officer and West Point graduate, achieving goals has been a way of life. Now, as a Chaplain in the United States Army Reserves, I face a myriad of competing priorities and schedules in my day-to-day ministry. I am a husband, father, youth pastor, and manager as well as a minister who proudly wears the Army uniform on weekends, or whenever the call arises to support our great nation. Collectively, these roles could overwhelm me, but God created me to serve him and the Soldiers placed in my care. I use the strength that God gave me as an Achiever to face these challenges with renewed vigor each and every day.

The Achiever strength enables me to diligently manage my to-do list. Creating, cataloging, managing, and completing the items on my list allows me to be productive and get the job done. Even though there are many competing demands on my time, I can still manage to find time to minister to Soldiers throughout the month. Managing the items on my lists gives me the focus to zero in on my responsibilities to my unit Commander, fellow ministry team members, and Soldiers, even when juggling my duties to my family, co-workers and church. In fact, I can transition from my weekly ministry to serving Soldiers and then back again because I wake up refreshed, re-energized, and ready to tackle the day's tasks, every morning. While completing tasks may seem an impersonal way to refer to ministry, it helps me to create space to carry out my pastoral role.

The life of an Achiever is illustrated well in Proverbs 31. Even though I am a man, I can still appreciate the incredible stamina that God gave this woman to be productive. In my own walk, the verse that speaks to me most is Philippians 4.13, "*I can do all things through him who strengthens me.*" (NKJV) (This verse was my mantra during an intense period of Army training called Ranger school.) I prayed, "Keep putting one foot in front of the other. Complete the next task. Jesus, you are the one who strengthens me for the tasks and challenges before me." It is in Christ's power that I can achieve and complete today's tasks.

Activator

Activator Strength Highlight – *People strong in the Activator theme can make things happen by turning thoughts into actions. They are often impatient.*

Scriptural Support for the Activator Strength

James 1.22-24 — Do not deceive yourselves by just listening to his word; instead, put it into practice. If you listen to the word, but do not put it into practice you are like people who look in a mirror and see themselves as they are. They take a good look at themselves and then go away and at once forget what they look like.

Ecclesiastes 11.4-6 — If you wait until the wind and the weather are just right, you will never plant anything and never harvest anything. God made everything, and you can no more understand what he does than you understand how new life begins in the womb of a pregnant woman. Do your planting in the morning and in the evening, too. You never know whether it will all grow well or whether one planting will do better than the other.

Nehemiah – Activating his Team

Nehemiah 2.9-18 — The emperor sent some army officers and a troop of cavalry with me, and I made the journey to West-of-Euphrates. There I gave the emperor's letters to the governors. But Sanballat, from the town of Beth Horon, and Tobiah, an official in the province of Ammon, heard that someone had come to work for the good of the people of Israel, and they were highly indignant. I went on to Jerusalem, and for three days I did not tell anyone what God had inspired me to do for Jerusalem. Then in the middle of the night I got up and went out, taking a few of my companions with me. The only animal we took was the donkey that I rode on. It was still night as I left the city through the Valley Gate on the west and went south past Dragon's Fountain to the Rubbish Gate. As I went, I inspected the broken walls of the city and the gates that had been destroyed by fire. Then on the east side of the city I went north to the Fountain Gate and the King's Pool. The donkey I was riding could not find any path through the rubble, so I went down into Kidron Valley and rode along, looking at the wall. Then I returned the way I had come and went back into the city through the Valley Gate. None of the local officials knew where I had gone or what I had been doing. So far I had not said anything to any of the other Jews — the priests, the leaders, the officials, or anyone else who would be taking part in the work. But now I said to them, "See what trouble we are in because Jerusalem is in ruins and its gates are destroyed! Let's rebuild the city walls and put an end to our disgrace." And I told them how God had been with me and helped me, and what the emperor had said to me. They responded, "Let's start rebuilding!" And they got ready to start the work.

Deeper Dive

- What things did Nehemiah use to spark the rebuilding of the walls?
- What do you think motivated Nehemiah the most to rebuild the walls?
- Do you face any major 'walls' that must be rebuilt in your life? What are they and how might faith in God help you confront them?
- How often do you want to do things now, rather than simply talk about doing them? Has your Activator talent ever prompted you to get people to take action? If so, describe what happened.

Challenge: Use your creative momentum, initiation, and instigation to move God's people.

Appreciation: Encourage those with the Activator talent to continue to bring a catalytic sense of urgency to help people get started and quickly do Kingdom work.

ENGAGE YOUR STRENGTHS STORIES

Hal Haller – *Church Planting Director for the Baptist Convention of New York*

Two words have characterized my life: starting and restarting. Whether starting a Christian group on a college campus, as a college student, or resurrecting a dying, dysfunctional youth ministry after seminary; or, starting a new church consulting company, or starting new churches in multiple locations, my joy and passion has always involved initiating something new. My energy and effort are best focused when I have a new project, new opportunity, new problem or new challenge to overcome. Fortunately, God has always put me in places and situations that have leveraged the gifts he has given me – and that has made me extremely content.

An Activator asks the question, "When can we start?" I like to get moving - make a decision, take action, look at the result and learn. There's no time to sit on my hands and overly think or talk about what needs to be done. My family, work team, and friends regularly comment that they love the explosion of energy, decisiveness, and boldness that I bring to getting something off the ground. This strength brings teamwork, focus, and immediate accomplishment. Since I have a tendency to be impatient, long meetings drain me, but action invigorates me! There's movement in my feet!

There are two characters in the Bible with whom I most resonate. The first is an Old Testament hero named Nehemiah who was undoubtedly an Activator. I have read his story dozens of times. His strength, determination, energy, team building/organization skills, and effort in the enormous task of rebuilding the wall in Jerusalem continue to inspire me. He built a wall that should have taken years to complete, in just 52 days! The second is the apostle Paul who wrote most of the New Testament. He was a catalytic missionary starting new churches across the Roman Empire. When describing his life mission, he said: "*My ambition has always been to preach the Good News where the name of Christ has never been heard, rather than where a church has already been started by someone else*" (Romans 15.20, NLT). Like the apostle Paul, my mission is to establish new beach heads for God's Kingdom so others might experience the joy of knowing Christ for the first time.

Adaptability

Adaptability Strength Highlight – *People strong in the Adaptability theme prefer to "go with the flow." They tend to be "now" people who take things as they come and discover the future one day at a time.*

Scriptural Support for the Adaptability Strength

Matthew 6.25-34 — "This is why I tell you: do not be worried about the food and drink you need in order to stay alive, or about clothes for your body. After all, isn't life worth more than food? And isn't the body worth more than clothes? Look at the birds: they do not plant seeds, gather a harvest and put it in barns; yet your Father in heaven takes care of them! Aren't you worth much more than birds? Can any of you live a bit longer by worrying about it? And why worry about clothes? Look how the wild flowers grow: they do not work or make clothes for themselves. But I tell you that not even King Solomon with all his wealth had clothes as beautiful as one of these flowers. It is God who clothes the wild grass — grass that is here today and gone tomorrow, burned up in the oven. Won't he be all the more sure to clothe you? What little faith you have! So do not start worrying: 'Where will my food come from? or my drink? or my clothes?' (These are the things the pagans are always concerned about.) Your Father in heaven knows that you need all these things. Instead, be concerned above everything else with the Kingdom of God and with what he requires of you, and he will provide you with all these other things. So do not worry about tomorrow; it will have enough worries of its own. There is no need to add to the troubles each day brings."

Abram – A Model of Adaptability*

Genesis 12.1-10 — The Lord said to Abram, "Leave your country, your relatives, and your father's home, and go to a land that I am going to show you. I will give you many descendants, and they will become a great nation. I will bless you and make your name famous, so that you will be a blessing. I will bless those who bless you, but I will curse those who curse you. And through you I will bless all the nations." When Abram was seventy-five years old, he started out from Haran, as the Lord had told him to do; and Lot went with him. Abram took his wife Sarai, his nephew Lot, and all the wealth and all the slaves they had acquired in Haran, and they started out for the land of Canaan. When they arrived in Canaan, Abram traveled through the land until he came to the sacred tree of Moreh, the holy place at Shechem. (At that time the Canaanites were still living in the land.) The Lord appeared to Abram and said to him, "This is the country that I am going to give to your descendants." Then Abram built an altar there to the Lord, who had appeared to him. After that, he moved on south to the hill country east of the city of Bethel and set up his camp between Bethel on the west and Ai on the east. There also he built an altar and worshiped the Lord. Then he moved on from place to place, going toward the southern part of Canaan. But there was a famine in Canaan, and it was so bad that Abram went farther south to Egypt, to live there for a while.

*God changed Abram's name to Abraham (Genesis 17.5) because he would be "the ancestor of many nations."

Deeper Dive

- Why do you think Abram was willing to leave his country and follow God's call? Have you ever experienced such a call? When?
- Are you facing a change in direction in your life? What is it and how might faith in God help you confront it?

- Does your Adaptability talent help you see the future as a place that you create out of the choices you make right now? If so, describe that process.

- How often do people describe you as a 'river,' with the ability to 'go with the flow'?

Challenge: Creative spontaneity, detours, and change in direction may provide opportunity for faith and obedience to grow while leading to God's blessing.

Appreciation: Encourage leaders with the Adaptability talent to continue to react with immediacy and a willingness to go where change takes you.

ENGAGE YOUR STRENGTHS STORIES

Kristi Leile Caterson – *Artist and Owner, LizaBelle Studios*

From as far back as I can remember, living in the moment, seemed like the natural thing to do. Spontaneity has never scared me, but rigid, strict predictability can at times be almost debilitating. I usually make a general plan for my day, my week or my month, but it's as though I make my plan knowing that at any moment, circumstances might change that could require me to be flexible.

I live for those moments. When things must shift and the pressure that shift presents demands my immediate response, I'm ready to react willingly to that change, even if it means that what I had planned for the day doesn't get accomplished. After all, there's always tomorrow!

I love taking detours. I look forward to the unexpected and I feel most productive when I am being pulled in many different directions at one time. It's almost like the tension of chaos ignites something in me, giving me energy to respond in a way that I wouldn't if there had been none. I gather strength from things that need my immediate attention. I understand that things are always in flux, organic, and that my role is to respond in the same way knowing that it will all happen as it should.

When I read the story of Abram in Genesis 12.1-10, I can definitely see his Adaptability at work. It reads: "*... they arrived in Canaan . . . After that, he moved on south to the hill country east of the city of Bethel and set up his camp between Bethel on the west and Ai on the east . . . Then he moved on from place to place, going toward the southern part of Canaan . . . Abram went farther south to Egypt, to live there for a while*" (Genesis 12.5b-10). No matter where the Lord directed Abram, he could go with the flow. Matthew 6.34 also concludes with solid support for being Adaptable, "*So do not worry about tomorrow; it will have enough worries of its own. There is no need to add to the troubles each day brings.*"

Analytical

Analytical Strength Highlight – *People strong in the Analytical theme search for reasons and causes. They have the ability to think about all the factors that might affect a situation.*

Scriptural Support for the Analytical Strength

Luke 14.28 — If one of you is planning to build a tower, you sit down first and figure out what it will cost, to see if you have enough money to finish the job.

John 20.24-29 — One of the twelve disciples, Thomas (called the Twin), was not with them when Jesus came. So the other disciples told him, "We have seen the Lord!" Thomas said to them, "Unless I see the scars of the nails in his hands and put my finger on those scars and my hand in his side, I will not believe." A week later the disciples were together again indoors, and Thomas was with them. The doors were locked, but Jesus came and stood among them and said, "Peace be with you." Then he said to Thomas, "Put your finger here, and look at my hands; then reach out your hand and put it in my side. Stop your doubting, and believe!" Thomas answered him, "My Lord and my God!" Jesus said to him, "Do you believe because you see me? How happy are those who believe without seeing me!"

Solomon and the Analytical Strength

1 Kings 3.5-15 — That night the Lord appeared to him in a dream and asked him, "What would you like me to give you?" Solomon answered, "You always showed great love for my father David, your servant, and he was good, loyal, and honest in his relation with you. And you have continued to show him your great and constant love by giving him a son who today rules in his place. O Lord God, you have let me succeed my father

as king, even though I am very young and don't know how to rule. Here I am among the people you have chosen to be your own, a people who are so many that they cannot be counted. So give me the wisdom I need to rule your people with justice and to know the difference between good and evil. Otherwise, how would I ever be able to rule this great people of yours?" The Lord was pleased that Solomon had asked for this, and so he said to him, "Because you have asked for the wisdom to rule justly, instead of long life for yourself or riches or the death of your enemies, I will do what you have asked. I will give you more wisdom and understanding than anyone has ever had before or will ever have again. I will also give you what you have not asked for: all your life you will have wealth and honor, more than that of any other king. And if you obey me and keep my laws and commands, as your father David did, I will give you a long life." Solomon woke up and realized that God had spoken to him in the dream. Then he went to Jerusalem and stood in front of the Lord's Covenant Box and offered burnt offerings and fellowship offerings to the Lord. After that he gave a feast for all his officials.

Deeper Dive

- What motivates Solomon to ask for wisdom?
- How does Solomon's Analytical approach impact his life and his people?
- Are there people who might benefit from the data and facts that you have been recently considering?
- Are there any emotionally charged issues facing your team that can use your logical, objective, dispassionate thinking?

Challenge: Use your Analytical talent to help a person or group that is struggling to organize a large body of information or bring structure to their ideas.

Appreciation: Give the Analytical person enough time to do a task correctly by checking with them as they progress. Adjust deadlines when possible.

ENGAGE YOUR STRENGTHS STORIES

John Greco – *Managing Director of Operations, Ministry Mobilization*

In navigating through the challenging waters of life, growing up with a penchant to take a closer look at things, observe people, test behaviors, listen carefully, and act methodically – has all served me very well. Those categorized as "analytical" in nature, like me, are often stigmatized as robotic, rigid or unforgiving; but, actually God offered the gift of being able to learn and discern to help people do the exact opposite. This is a strength that has enabled me to remain realistic regarding options and consequences in all things I face, whether they be professional or personal, and also assess all options for resolution to make the best choices accordingly.

Analysis empowers us. I have always felt this way and, as I get older, I have seen countless examples of it as an essential way to grow and continue to engage well with others. Actually, engaging this internal strength enables me to develop external strengths in relationships and in carving the best way forward in all I do. This does not mean that every situation warrants the same level of research or measurement, but this approach and core discipline of analysis must take root. It is just as important to understand why a problem has arisen as it is to craft potential solutions to address that problem. Without this methodology, the problem has a very good chance of cropping up again, and/ or taking on a variance of shape. Therefore, the importance of the source of each issue or challenge cannot be underestimated. I love facts and figures, but I love providing clarity and serving others more so - with the in-depth application of those tools to get jobs done well and progress.

In my professional role in Operations, I am able to leverage this strength that the Lord has provided me in addressing all challenges that face my colleagues and threaten the goals that we are so deeply committed to achieving as a team. Managing resources: personnel, budgets, technology and data, enable me to have comprehensive pictures of the current state and forthcoming challenges, as well as to propose best practices and solutions to achieve goals. My daily work demands I live simultaneously in two worlds: "high-level vision" as well as "the nuts and bolts." Through an analytical eye, I weave these two together to map out the best road for the team. Being analytical and taking this core approach becomes a standard filter for addressing all tasks presented to me. In taking this approach, I am often reminded of 1 Kings 3.5-15, in which Solomon asks the Lord for the essential tool of understanding required to lead God's people. That is the beauty of the God-given strength of being Analytical – it enables you to put understanding to use in helping others.

Arranger

Arranger Strength Highlight – *People strong in the Arranger theme can organize, but they also have a flexibility that complements this ability. They like to figure out how all of the pieces and resources can be arranged for maximum productivity.*

Scriptural Support for the Arranger Strength

Psalm 8.4-6 — What are human beings, that you think of them; mere mortals, that you care for them? Yet you made them inferior only to yourself; you crowned them with glory and honor. You appointed them rulers over everything you made; you placed them over all creation.

Proverbs 15.22 — Get all the advice you can, and you will succeed; without it you will fail.

1 Corinthians 12.18 — As it is, however, God put every different part in the body just as he wanted it to be.

Jethro's Arranger Strength Helps Moses

Exodus 18.13-26 — The next day Moses was settling disputes among the people, and he was kept busy from morning till night. When Jethro saw everything that Moses had to do, he asked, "What is all this that you are doing for the people? Why are you doing this all alone, with people standing here from morning till night to consult you?" Moses answered, "I must do this because the people come to me to learn God's will. When two people have a dispute, they come to me, and I decide which one of them is right, and I tell them God's commands and laws." Then Jethro said, "You are not doing this right. You will wear yourself out and these people as well. This is too much for you to do alone. Now let me give you some good advice, and God will be with you. It is right for you to represent the people before God and bring their disputes to him. You should teach them God's commands and explain to them how they should live and what they should do. But in addition, you should choose some capable men and appoint them as leaders of the people: leaders of thousands, hundreds, fifties, and tens. They must be God-fearing men who can be trusted and who cannot be bribed. Let them serve as judges for the people on a permanent basis. They can bring all the difficult cases to you, but they themselves can decide all the smaller disputes. That will make it easier for you, as they share your burden. If you do this, as God commands, you will not wear yourself out, and all these people can go home with their disputes settled." Moses took Jethro's advice and chose capable men from among all the Israelites. He appointed them as leaders of thousands, hundreds, fifties, and tens. They served as judges for the people on a permanent basis, bringing the difficult cases to Moses but deciding the smaller disputes themselves.

Deeper Dive

- Jethro celebrates the accomplishments of God with Moses earlier in the chapter. How is it that he can then confront Moses about the way in which he was settling disputes among the people? What does this tell us?
- How does Jethro confront Moses? What is important about the way that he does it?
- List all the elements that Jethro considers and uses to make Moses' task more efficient.
- How can we apply Jethro's example to increase efficiency or production in our ministry?

Challenge: Use your Arranger ability to assess, advise and manage a better way forward.

Appreciation: Help an Arranger do what they do best – organize complex situations. Be open-minded and support their efforts to bring efficiency to our Kingdom efforts.

ENGAGE YOUR STRENGTHS STORIES

Beth Mills—*Wife, Mom, Leader, Mentor, PWOC Leader*

When I was in high school, I was the drum major in our marching band. We spent hours studying marching charts and musical scores, learning and rehearsing routines that started out looking and feeling like mass chaos. It takes incredible teamwork for all those people to create a kaleidoscopic display, lines moving in and out and curving around one another on the field, all while playing instruments and marching to the rhythm of the drum line. I loved every minute of it, especially when the mess turned into the marching masterpiece.

I've used the skills I learned as a drum major many times through the years, leveraging my strength as an Arranger. I'm a homeschooling mom of five children, all born in a 6½ year span. I was always creating and improving new activity schedules, chore charts, homeschooling schedules, and progress reports for our very active family. With each new semester and with every military move, I was constantly saying, "How can we do this more efficiently?" and "There's got to be a better way."

For the most part, we embraced change because it held the promise of the new and better way to homeschool successfully. I've also coordinated training for 150 military installations worldwide to receive resources and training for vibrant women's ministry. The challenges of matching lead trainers with new trainers and with the needs of the different installations, keeping in mind the travel required all while staying within our budget, made my heart race--not with stress, but with excitement. I was made for this! Our greatest challenge came when I was president of the ministry and we reorganized our infrastructure in order to cut our budget in half while maintaining the excellent training and resourcing needed to sustain a healthy women's ministry.

My heart especially goes out to women who are exhausted, trying to keep up with so many schedules, responsibilities, and busy families. When Jethro visited Moses in the desert, he gave Moses excellent leadership advice and a plan for organizing the Israelites for maximum effectiveness. He prefaced the plan with the reason: "*...You are not doing this right. You will wear yourself out and these people as well*" (Exodus 18:17, 18a). Whether I'm advising women's ministry teams or if I'm mentoring women one on one, I'm on the lookout for ways to rearrange the pieces and simplify the process so life-giving ministry can occur without "wearing ourselves out" on the way.

Belief

Belief Strength Highlight — *People strong in the Belief theme have certain core values that are unchanging. Out of these values emerges a defined purpose for their life.*

Scriptural Support for the Belief Strength

Matthew 28.18-20 — Jesus drew near and said to them, "I have been given all authority in heaven and on earth. Go, then, to all peoples everywhere and make them my disciples: baptize them in the name of the Father, the Son, and the Holy Spirit, and teach them to obey everything I have commanded you. And I will be with you always, to the end of the age."

John 20.27-29 — Then he said to Thomas, "Put your finger here, and look at my hands; then reach out your hand and put it in my side. Stop your doubting, and believe!" Thomas answered him, "My Lord and my God!" Jesus said to him, "Do you believe because you see me? How happy are those who believe without seeing me!"

Joshua's Belief Statement

Joshua 24.14-27 — "Now then," Joshua continued, "honor the Lord and serve him sincerely and faithfully. Get rid of the gods which your ancestors used to worship in Mesopotamia and in Egypt, and serve only the Lord. If you are not willing to serve him, decide today whom you will serve, the gods your ancestors worshiped in Mesopotamia or the gods of the Amorites, in whose land you are now living. As for my family and me, we will serve the Lord." The people replied, "We would never leave the Lord to serve other gods! The Lord our God brought our fathers and us out of slavery in Egypt, and we saw the miracles that he performed. He kept us safe wherever we went among all the nations through which we passed.

As we advanced into this land, the Lord drove out all the Amorites who lived here. So we also will serve the Lord; he is our God." Joshua said to the people, "But you may not be able to serve the Lord. He is a holy God and will not forgive your sins. He will tolerate no rivals, and if you leave him to serve foreign gods, he will turn against you and punish you. He will destroy you, even though he was good to you before." The people said to Joshua, "No! We will serve the Lord." Joshua told them, "You are your own witnesses to the fact that you have chosen to serve the Lord." "Yes," they said, "we are witnesses." "Then get rid of those foreign gods that you have," he demanded, "and pledge your loyalty to the Lord, the God of Israel." The people then said to Joshua, "We will serve the Lord our God. We will obey his commands." So Joshua made a covenant for the people that day, and there at Shechem he gave them laws and rules to follow. Joshua wrote these commands in the book of the Law of God. Then he took a large stone and set it up under the oak tree in the Lord's sanctuary. He said to all the people, "This stone will be our witness. It has heard all the words that the Lord has spoken to us. So it will be a witness against you, to keep you from rebelling against your God."

Deeper Dive

- What does Joshua's belief in an all-powerful God communicate to those around him?
- In what manner did Joshua correspond with the Israelites? How did the people respond to Joshua's belief?
- Why did Joshua enter into a covenant with the people? How did he do it? Why is this important?
- How can we use our belief in the almighty Lord to lift up and edify the Church on earth?

Challenge: Let your zeal for what is right before God shine before others.

Appreciation: Encourage someone with godly convictions to share them with others so that we might continue to build up the Kingdom of God.

ENGAGE YOUR STRENGTHS STORIES

Darah Wilson—*Gallup® Certified StrengthsFinder® Coach*

Everyone has thoughts about what is true. For some people, truth resonates stronger than in others. When I was two years old, my mom recounts the moment she realized she had a very "opinionated" little girl with particular demands. Actually, I was expressing my Belief strength…I *believed* that wearing stripes, polka dots, and rain boots was a great look! Now, as a leader in ministry and missions, my belief guides and allows me to execute tasks successfully in countless Kingdom-focused roles and opportunities. As a professional coach, mentor, passionate friend, family member, and peer, I cannot ignore the innate desire to express my own beliefs in an effort to persuade others.

My Belief is expressed through the very deeply-held and unwavering ideas I have about what is true. I'm not easily influenced by others, especially when it comes to my values. Once I have good reason to believe in something, it can be nearly impossible to convince me otherwise. Old friends marvel at my ability to "remain the same person" with maturing, but unchanging convictions, no matter how much time has passed.

In ministry, when faced with unglamorous and menial tasks, my Belief is the fuel that motivates me to persevere and to finish what I start. Even in the most challenging circumstances that tempt me to quit, my belief continually reminds me "this is why you're doing this." When involved in something about which I truly believe, I'll be an advocate with unrivaled drive and motivation. On the other hand, I find it near impossible to work toward something in which I see little purpose or meaning. I can't separate a "job" and a "calling." Investing time and energy into anything requires that it be connected to my strong Belief, and "success" for me is much more than money and prestige.

I love the passion and zeal Joshua brought forth as a leader and steadfast follower of God. In Joshua 24, when entrusted with the responsibility to bring conviction to the people, he starts by expressing the fact that he and his house will serve the Lord. That wasn't enough. He had to bring others along. He demands their understanding and response to the fact that serving other gods was ABSOLUTELY UNACCEPTABLE. Their first agreeable response was not enough for Joshua. He continued on, expressing the depravity of what it would mean should they turn back to their gods. His strong Belief impacted them so greatly that God's Word reports, "*Israel served the Lord all the days of Joshua*" (Joshua 24.31, ESV).

Command

> **Command Strength Highlight** – *People strong in the Command theme have presence. They can take control of a situation and make decisions.*

Scriptural Support for the Command Strength

Exodus 5.1 — Then Moses and Aaron went to the king of Egypt and said, "The Lord, the God of Israel, says, 'Let my people go, so that they can hold a festival in the desert to honor me.'"

1 Samuel 17.37 — David said, "The Lord has saved me from lions and bears; he will save me from this Philistine."

Ephesians 4.25-27 — No more lying, then! Each of you must tell the truth to the other believer, because we are all members together in the body of Christ. If you become angry, do not let your anger lead you into sin, and do not stay angry all day. Don't give the Devil a chance.

Jesus – Taking Charge

John 2.13-22 — It was almost time for the Passover Festival, so Jesus went to Jerusalem. There in the Temple he found people selling cattle, sheep, and pigeons, and also the moneychangers sitting at their tables. So he made a whip from cords and drove all the animals out of the Temple, both the sheep and the cattle; he overturned the tables of the moneychangers and scattered their coins; and he ordered those who sold the pigeons, "Take them out of here! Stop making my Father's house a marketplace!" His disciples remembered that the Scripture says, "My devotion to your house, O God, burns in me like a fire." The Jewish authorities came back at him with a question, "What miracle can you perform to show us that you have the right to do this?" Jesus answered, "Tear down this Temple, and in three days I will build it again." "Are you going to build it again in three days?" they asked him. "It has taken forty-six years to build this Temple!" But the temple Jesus was speaking about was his body. So when he was raised from death, his disciples remembered that he had said this, and they believed the Scripture and what Jesus had said.

Deeper Dive

- What does Jesus see when He enters the Temple? Why is Jesus enraged by what He sees?
- What does Jesus do to bring the situation back to proper order?
- What can we do to bring an out of control situation back to order? Who can help?
- How can our use of Command help restore Kingdom living?

Challenge: Explain to others how you can take action that brings order to an out of control situation.

Appreciation: Encourage a person with Command to be direct and succinct when they communicate what needs to be done.

ENGAGE YOUR STRENGTHS STORIES

Kristy McAdams—*Coach and Strengths Development Specialist*

When I was a little girl, my grandfather used to tell me he thought I would be an attorney when I grew up. When I asked him why, he said that I made convincing arguments. I didn't understand until many years later that he saw an unusual clarity and strength in our conversations. While I am not an attorney, Command has taken me places in life that I wouldn't have gone without it. I've worked with ministries, had various leadership roles, and have taken on challenges with confidence. As a mom, I've relied on my Command many times to get through to my stubborn and rebellious son. When I'm in full Command mode, he listens. Command brings courage that allows me to make hard choices and forge ahead when it seems impossible to move a step further. Some people have said that I'm brave, but I don't feel that way because command has always been part of me. In stressful situations, my Command strength quickly comes to attention with tremendous emotional clarity. I instinctively understand what needs to be done for the well-being of everyone involved, and how to communicate so that we all move together.

How I impact others factors into my choices because people matter to me, and relationships are so important. I like to get to the heart of matters, put everything on the table, and work through problems when they come up. My instinct is to clear the path so that we can move forward together. Things that are hidden tend to cause problems later. If we can be honest with each other, we can stay connected. When I'm focused on what we need to do, I have to be careful about how I express myself because my Command causes me to speak with authority. There have been times that I've unintentionally intimidated others because my statements were too strong.

Because *Engage Your Strengths* has helped me learn how to manage my Command, I'm aware that I impact others not just with my words, but also with authority. Jesus was a perfect example of how to best use Command. John 2.15-16 explains that when moneychangers were in the temple, Jesus overturned their tables and said, "*Take them out of here! Stop making my Father's house a marketplace!*" (v 16). Jesus boldly protected ordinary people from the moneychangers who were taking advantage of them.

Communication

> **Communication Strength Highlight** – *People strong in the Communication theme generally find it easy to put their thoughts into words. They are good conversationalists and presenters.*

Scriptural Support for the Communication Strength

Ecclesiastes 12.9-11 — But because the Philosopher was wise, he kept on teaching the people what he knew. He studied proverbs and honestly tested their truth. The Philosopher tried to find comforting words, but the words he wrote were honest. The sayings of the wise are like the sharp sticks that shepherds use to guide sheep, and collected proverbs are as lasting as firmly driven nails. They have been given by God, the one Shepherd of us all.

Matthew 7.28, 29 — When Jesus finished saying these things, the crowd was amazed at the way he taught. He wasn't like the teachers of the Law; instead, he taught with authority.

Romans 10.14, 15 — But how can they call to him for help if they have not believed? And how can they believe if they have not heard the message? And how can they hear if the message is not proclaimed? And how can the message be proclaimed if the messengers are not sent out? As the Scripture says, "How wonderful is the coming of messengers who bring good news!"

Aaron – Communication Strength

Exodus 4.10-17, 27-31 — But Moses said, "No, Lord, don't send me. I have never been a good speaker, and I haven't become one since you began to speak to me. I am a poor speaker, slow and hesitant." The Lord said to him, "Who gives man his mouth? Who makes him deaf or dumb? Who gives him sight or makes him blind? It is I, the Lord. Now, go! I will help you to speak, and I will tell you what to say." But Moses answered, "No, Lord, please send someone else." At this the Lord became angry with Moses and said, "What about your brother Aaron, the Levite? I know that he can speak well. In fact, he is now coming to meet you and will be glad to see you. You can speak to him and tell him what to say. I will help both of you to speak, and I will tell you both what to do. He will be your spokesman and speak to the people for you. Then you will be like God, telling him what to say. Take this walking stick with you; for with it you will perform miracles." . . . Meanwhile the Lord had said to Aaron, "Go into the desert to meet Moses." So he went to meet him at the holy mountain; and when he met him, he kissed him. Then Moses told Aaron everything that the Lord had said when he told him to return to Egypt; he also told him about the miracles which the Lord had ordered him to perform. So Moses and Aaron went to Egypt and gathered all the Israelite leaders together. Aaron told them everything that the Lord had said to Moses, and then Moses performed all the miracles in front of the people. They believed, and when they heard that the Lord had come to them and had seen how they were being treated cruelly, they bowed down and worshiped.

Deeper Dive

- What do you think caused Aaron to step up to be used as God's mouthpiece? Have you ever experienced that same call? When?
- Like Moses, are there things that you are not good at that make you feel inadequate? How might collaborating with another person help you confront them?
- Has your Communication talent ever prompted you to tell a story to help others understand God's message? If so, briefly retell the story.
- How does talking things out edify a group and bring understanding to a discussion?

Challenge: Use creative stories and storytellers to capture and draw people to God and God's message and miracles.

Appreciation: Encourage those with the Communication talent to explain, host, speak, write and bring ideas and events to life – making them vivid and exciting!

ENGAGE YOUR STRENGTHS STORIES

Jim Young—*Web Creative Director*

When you and I consciously embrace our strengths, not only do we garner greater self-awareness, but we also begin to see our roles and responsibilities in life with a higher level of focus and intention. As a Christian, husband, father of five, creative director, scout cubmaster, and teacher within the local church, I am often amazed - and simultaneously grateful - for the opportunities to articulate ideas that inform and inspire those within my spheres of influence – beginning with my family and beyond to the larger community. There is an energy that borders on the miraculous no matter what responsibility I am undertaking when I lean into my strengths.

I am presented with opportunities on a consistent basis to express ideas and principles with clarity - whether to a large group in a teaching setting, or a single person over the phone. When connecting with people in a church class setting, I am able to articulate biblical principles and stories that inform, empower, and inspire each person to realize their God-given potential within the body of Christ and discover their place of service. Possessing an inherent ability to engage an audience, I am able to captivate eighty of the finest 5- to 10- year old young boys in order to communicate core values of scouting with simple, memorable principles that help these young scouts recall them and apply them to their life. With my children, I will often play the role of "talk show host" in order to engage them in fun conversations about who they are. This can lead to a discussion that solidifies the biblical values that God desires to instill in them. Last, and probably most important, I nurture a stronger relationship with my wife when I am able to express in words her value as a person and role in our family, or reiterate her frustrations so I clearly understand her needs and how I might be able to serve her with greater intention.

I don't believe a greater communicator has ever existed than the Lord Jesus himself. As evidenced in Matthew 7.28-29: "*When Jesus finished saying these things, the crowd was amazed at the way he taught. He wasn't like the teachers of the Law; instead, he taught with authority.*" Jesus' words have had the greatest impact on the world than the words of any other, and he is the example for those of us in whom God has planted the gift of communication. We're possessors of a gift that - if we steward intentionally and with humility - will nurture lasting relationships, transfer ideas and stories with clarity, and, by God's grace, transform the lives of people!

Competition

Competition Strength Highlight — *People strong in the Competition theme measure their progress against the performance of others. They strive to win first place and revel in contests. (They can energize others to move to higher levels of excellence.)*

Scriptural Support for the Competition Strength

1 Corinthians 9.24-26a — Surely you know that many runners take part in a race, but only one of them wins the prize. Run, then, in such a way as to win the prize. Every athlete in training submits to strict discipline, in order to be crowned with a wreath that will not last; but we do it for one that will last forever. That is why I run straight for the finish line.

David Demonstrates the Competition Strength

1 Samuel 17.24-37a; 40-47 — When the Israelites saw Goliath, they ran away in terror. "Look at him!" they said to each other. "Listen to his challenge! King Saul has promised to give a big reward to the man who kills him; the king will also give him his daughter to marry and will not require his father's family to pay taxes." David asked the men who were near him, "What will the man get who kills this Philistine and frees Israel from this disgrace? After all, who is this heathen Philistine to defy the army of the living God?" They told him what would be done for the man who killed Goliath. Eliab, David's oldest brother, heard David talking to the men. He became angry with David and said, "What are you doing here? Who is taking care of those sheep of yours out there in the wilderness? You smart aleck, you! You just came to watch the fighting!" "Now what have I done?" David asked. "Can't I even ask a question?" He turned to another man and asked him the same question, and every time he asked, he got the same answer. Some men heard what David had said, and they told Saul, who

sent for him. David said to Saul, "Your Majesty, no one should be afraid of this Philistine! I will go and fight him." "No," answered Saul. "How could you fight him? You're just a boy, and he has been a soldier all his life!" "Your Majesty," David said, "I take care of my father's sheep. Any time a lion or a bear carries off a lamb, I go after it, attack it, and rescue the lamb. And if the lion or bear turns on me, I grab it by the throat and beat it to death. I have killed lions and bears, and I will do the same to this heathen Philistine, who has defied the army of the living God. The Lord has saved me from lions and bears; he will save me from this Philistine." . . . He took his shepherd's stick and then picked up five smooth stones from the stream and put them in his bag. With his sling ready, he went out to meet Goliath. The Philistine started walking toward David, with his shield bearer walking in front of him. He kept coming closer, and when he got a good look at David, he was filled with scorn for him because he was just a nice, good-looking boy. He said to David, "What's that stick for? Do you think I'm a dog?" And he called down curses from his god on David. "Come on," he challenged David, "and I will give your body to the birds and animals to eat." David answered, "You are coming against me with sword, spear, and javelin, but I come against you in the name of the Lord Almighty, the God of the Israelite armies, which you have defied. This very day the Lord will put you in my power; I will defeat you and cut off your head. And I will give the bodies of the Philistine soldiers to the birds and animals to eat. Then the whole world will know that Israel has a God, and everyone here will see that the Lord does not need swords or spears to save his people. He is victorious in battle, and he will put all of you in our power."

Deeper Dive

- What do you think really motivated David to challenge Goliath? Have you ever experienced that same motivation? When?
- Do you face any "Goliaths" in your life? What are they and how might faith in God help you confront them?

- Has your Competition talent ever prompted you to respond to a challenge? If so, describe the contest.
- How often do you get the chance to go against the best?

Challenge: Love competing and trust God for the victory.

Appreciation: Enjoy those with the Competition talent and encourage them to strive to win the things of the Kingdom of God.

ENGAGE YOUR STRENGTHS STORIES

Mark J. Won—*Chaplain, U.S. Navy*

I never imagined I would be serving as a U.S. Navy Chaplain. Growing up, I always imagined my profession would be more creative or competitive in sports. Now, as a husband, father of four children, and caregiver to Sailors, Marines, and Coastguardsmen, I have to find ways to creatively integrate my calling and gifts. There is no ideal Chaplain or Staff Officer. It's been a journey toward personal congruence--finding ways to express my unique personality and gifts, while meeting the needs of those entrusted to my care and exhibiting the professional competence expected from the institution. The StrengthsFinder® tools have been instrumental in this process.

The more I trained others, the more I became convinced to better engage my own strengths as a Competitor. Until *Engage Your Strengths*, I only perceived competition and comparison negatively. Now, knowing my strength has made me highly intentional about personal growth and reaching new professional goals as a Competitor. I have shared the Strengths paradigm with just about everyone, both at home and at work. I believe in it because it works. The language of Strengths made it possible for me to speak constructively with a disgruntled Sailor.

When he saw that I took a genuine interest in him and did not speak of his shortcomings, but about his potential, the young Sailor was very receptive. I was competing against this young Sailor's previous experiences with incompetent and weak leaders. The desire to turn the Sailor around was fueled by my competitive theme. Furthermore, the tool makes it possible to communicate with others in a team that your interest is their long-term growth, both personally and professionally. I would often say to those I train, "This is a tool for life...you will take it with you beyond this job. It is an investment in you as a person and not simply as an employee of an organization."

King David wrote, "*I will give thanks to You, for I am fearfully and wonderfully made; Wonderful are Your works, and my soul knows it very well*" (Psalm 139.14, NASB). There is a mystery and vastness to God's creation. At the pinnacle of this wonder is humanity. Made in God's image, our history books capture the irony of both transcendent and tyrannical figures that shaped the world in which they lived. Socrates is credited with saying, the "unobserved life is not worth living." *Engage Your Strengths* is a way to increase self-knowledge and reflection. It's a tool that has helped me plunge into the depths of who I am, with greater measure of confidence and assurance. To that end, it has helped me be more of who I am while shedding less of who I am not.

Connectedness

Connectedness Strength Highlight – *People strong in the Connectedness theme have faith in the links between all things. They believe there are few coincidences and that almost every event has a reason.*

Scriptural Support for the Connectedness Strength

Genesis 45.3-8 — Joseph said to his brothers, "I am Joseph. Is my father still alive?" But when his brothers heard this, they were so terrified that they could not answer. Then Joseph said to them, "Please come closer." They did, and he said, "I am your brother Joseph, whom you sold into Egypt. Now do not be upset or blame yourselves because you sold me here. It was really God who sent me ahead of you to save people's lives. This is only the second year of famine in the land; there will be five more years in which there will be neither plowing nor reaping. God sent me ahead of you to rescue you in this amazing way and to make sure that you and your descendants survive. So it was not really you who sent me here, but God. He has made me the king's highest official. I am in charge of his whole country; I am the ruler of all Egypt.

Hebrews 11.1-3 —To have faith is to be sure of the things we hope for, to be certain of the things we cannot see. It was by their faith that people of ancient times won God's approval. It is by faith that we understand that the universe was created by God's word, so that what can be seen was made out of what cannot be seen.

Romans 8.38, 39 — For I am certain that nothing can separate us from his love: neither death nor life, neither angels nor other heavenly rulers or powers, neither the present nor the future, neither the world above nor the world below — there is nothing in all creation that will ever be able to separate us from the love of God which is ours through Christ Jesus our Lord.

Connectedness and the Body

1 Corinthians 12.18-27 — As it is, however, God put every different part in the body just as he wanted it to be. There would not be a body if it were all only one part! As it is, there are many parts but one body. So then, the eye cannot say to the hand, "I don't need you!" Nor can the head say to the feet, "Well, I don't need you!" On the contrary, we cannot do without the parts of the body that seem to be weaker; and those parts that we think aren't worth very much are the ones which we treat with greater care; while the parts of the body which don't look very nice are treated with special modesty, which the more beautiful parts do not need. God himself has put the body together in such a way as to give greater honor to those parts that need it. And so there is no division in the body, but all its different parts have the same concern for one another. If one part of the body suffers, all the other parts suffer with it; if one part is praised, all the other parts share its happiness. All of you are Christ's body, and each one is a part of it.

Deeper Dive

- Why do you think Paul used the human body to illustrate our connectedness to Christ? What other things could he have used to make his point?
- In what way does Paul's allusion help us grasp the mystery of the body of Christ?
- Has your Connectedness talent ever caused people to think you were philosophical? If so, describe the conversation.
- How often do you get the chance to be part of something bigger than yourself?

Challenge: Help others see the interconnectedness of God's hand in our lives and relationships.

Appreciation: Ask those with Connectedness how they see God working in and around your difficult situations.

ENGAGE YOUR STRENGTHS STORIES

Mike Dugal— *Chaplain, U.S. Army*

As a young child, I remember walking through the woods and fields of Southeast Missouri tapping into my Native American heritage by witnessing and sensing creation's majesty and uniqueness. I would lay in the open fields by myself, knowing deep within that I was a part of the greater picture. Life challenges and situations were always viewed as part of a greater plan, as my mother reminded me of God's benevolent care and sovereignty. Always looking for the deeper purpose provided hope in the darkest of times. I tackled life knowing full well that all things worked together, even before I knew Romans 8.28.

StrengthsFinder®*s* provided a unique vocabulary allowing me to express, share, and defend who God had created me to be from a strength perspective. I was first introduced to StrengthsFinder®*s* while I was the Director of the Center for Spiritual Leadership for the Army Chaplaincy. In recording my life's journey, I quickly understood the ease with which I would connect with others, especially those who did not mirror my ethnicity, culture, faith, gender or worldview. My natural ability to build bridges with those who were different provided a sense of belonging in my life. My roles as husband, father, counselor, chaplain, administrator, adjunct professor, mentor, faith coach and Christ follower persistently complements the other. Connectedness allows me to live my life in a highly congruent manner with my close friends and colleagues. My life is an amazing and wonderful adventure being revealed moment by moment.

The Scripture text that establishes my understanding of Connectedness is Genesis 45.4-8a, where Joseph's dialogue with his brothers is recorded: "*I am your brother Joseph, whom you sold into Egypt. Now do not be upset or blame yourselves because you sold me here. It was really God who sent me ahead of you to save people's lives . . . God sent me ahead of you to rescue you in this amazing way and to make sure that you and your descendants survive. So it was not really you who sent me here, but God.*" Time and again I draw strength and assurance, in the midst of perceived chaos, that God is in control, he has a plan, his ways are trustworthy, and he is the one who directs my steps. The character and attributes of God are the foundations for Connectedness.

Consistency

> **Consistency Strength Highlight** – *People strong in the Consistency theme are keenly aware of the need to treat people the same. They try to treat everyone in the world with consistency by setting up clear rules and adhering to them.*

Scriptural Support for the Consistency Strength

Matthew 5.45b — For he makes his sun to shine on bad and good people alike, and gives rain to those who do good and to those who do evil.

Romans 12.3 — And because of God's gracious gift to me I say to every one of you: Do not think of yourself more highly than you should. Instead, be modest in your thinking, and judge yourself according to the amount of faith that God has given you.

Galatians 3.28 — So there is no difference between Jews and Gentiles, between slaves and free people, between men and women; you are all one in union with Christ Jesus.

Ephesians 4.4-6 — There is one body and one Spirit, just as there is one hope to which God has called you. There is one Lord, one faith, one baptism; there is one God and Father of all people, who is Lord of all, works through all, and is in all.

James Addresses Consistency

James 2.1-10 — My friends, as believers in our Lord Jesus Christ, the Lord of glory, you must never treat people in different ways according to their outward appearance. Suppose a rich man wearing a gold ring and fine clothes comes to your meeting, and a poor man in ragged clothes also comes. If you show more respect to the well-dressed man and say to him,

"Have this best seat here," but say to the poor man, "Stand over there, or sit here on the floor by my feet," then you are guilty of creating distinctions among yourselves and of making judgments based on evil motives. Listen, my dear friends! God chose the poor people of this world to be rich in faith and to possess the kingdom which he promised to those who love him. But you dishonor the poor! Who are the ones who oppress you and drag you before the judges? The rich! They are the ones who speak evil of that good name which has been given to you. You will be doing the right thing if you obey the law of the Kingdom, which is found in the Scripture, "Love your neighbor as you love yourself." But if you treat people according to their outward appearance, you are guilty of sin, and the Law condemns you as a lawbreaker. Whoever breaks one commandment is guilty of breaking them all.

Deeper Dive

- Why does James admonish us to be wary of showing partiality? Why is it sin to judge a person based on their external image?
- How does being partial to something differ from discernment?
- Why do you think that God chooses to confound the wisdom of this world?
- What are some ways that we can attempt to avoid partiality and favoritism?

Challenge: Use your gift of consistency to uphold biblical values inside and outside the church.

Appreciation: Thank someone who shows a consistent approach to people, problem solving, and the peace that it brings.

ENGAGE YOUR STRENGTHS STORIES

Dulce Alvarado—*Program/Project Manager, Nida Institute for Biblical Scholarship*

As a Program Manager, I am tasked with the administration, operations and financial responsibilities of the Nida Institute—the research, scholarship and service arm of American Bible Society. I've been working at American Bible Society for 15 years, most recently working in the Nida Institute for the past seven. I enjoy the challenge of ensuring that our staff complies with internal/corporate policies and trust that this is where God wants me to be at this point in my career. I am also a mom, step-mom and wife. It is important to me that I treat my daughter and stepson equally. It is the only way I assure that my family will treat others with respect.

Consistency gives me the opportunity to enforce the rules both at work and at home. For example, I have been affectionately referred to as a "drill sergeant" when it comes to approving expense reports. If there is something wrong with an expense report, I will not make exceptions, no matter the staff's title or influence in the organization. This may seem rigid and inflexible, but if these are the rules and regulations, who am I to make exceptions? It is this same strength that has helped me to create a work/life balance and routine for my family, and establish the good habits and behavior needed in today's society.

Being raised in the Catholic tradition, I was taught that God loves everyone equally. When the apostle James addresses consistency, he states: "*My friends, as believers in our Lord Jesus Christ, the Lord of glory, you must never treat people in different ways according to their outward appearance*" (James 2.1). The verse that most resonates with me is

Galatians 3.28 "*So there's no difference between Jews and Gentiles, between slaves and free people, between men and women; you are all in union with Christ Jesus.*" If we keep this in mind in our daily interactions, it will help us when we are challenged to make the right decision.

Context

Context Strength Highlight – *People strong in the Context theme enjoy thinking about the past. They understand the present by researching its history.*

Scriptural Support for the Context Strength

1 Samuel 12.6, 7 — Samuel continued, "The Lord is the one who chose Moses and Aaron and who brought your ancestors out of Egypt. Now stand where you are, and I will accuse you before the Lord by reminding you of all the mighty actions the Lord did to save you and your ancestors."

Ecclesiastes 3.15 — Whatever happens or can happen has already happened before. God makes the same thing happen again and again.

Hebrews 1.1, 2 — In the past God spoke to our ancestors many times and in many ways through the prophets, but in these last days he has spoken to us through his Son. He is the one through whom God created the universe, the one whom God has chosen to possess all things at the end.

Context Strength in Deuteronomy

Deuteronomy 4.1-10 — Then Moses said to the people, "Obey all the laws that I am teaching you, and you will live and occupy the land which the Lord, the God of your ancestors, is giving you. Do not add anything to what I command you, and do not take anything away. Obey the commands of the Lord your God that I have given you. You yourselves saw what the Lord did at Mount Peor. He destroyed everyone who worshiped Baal there, but those of you who were faithful to the Lord your God are still alive today. I have taught you all the laws, as the Lord my God told me to do. Obey them in the land that you are about to invade and occupy.

Obey them faithfully, and this will show the people of other nations how wise you are. When they hear of all these laws, they will say, 'What wisdom and understanding this great nation has!' No other nation, no matter how great, has a god who is so near when they need him as the Lord our God is to us. He answers us whenever we call for help. No other nation, no matter how great, has laws so just as those that I have taught you today. Be on your guard! Make certain that you do not forget, as long as you live, what you have seen with your own eyes. Tell your children and your grandchildren about the day you stood in the presence of the Lord your God at Mount Sinai, when he said to me, 'Assemble the people. I want them to hear what I have to say, so that they will learn to obey me as long as they live and so that they will teach their children to do the same.'"

Deeper Dive

- How does Moses help God's people learn from the past in order to move forward?
- Why does Moses emphasize God's law to the Israelites? What is the relationship between remembering the law and obedience?
- How does reflecting on God's past work help us understand what he wants us to do in the present?
- What is the proper use of tradition or history in a group or organization?
  How can you help your group learn from the past?

Challenge: Use your ability to understand God's present work based on what he has done in the past to connect people's stories with God's story.

Appreciation: Encourage a person with Context to strengthen the culture of your organization by researching and presenting how the best of its past informs its present goals and values.

ENGAGE YOUR STRENGTHS STORIES

Ken Bush—*Minister, Former Chaplain, U.S. Army*

As a former Army Officer with over 35 years of service, including 25 years as a Chaplain, I often served in positions that required the ability to quickly assess people and issues, and to develop and implement plans to move the organization forward. In addition, I was often asked to serve in the role of a strategic thinker, analyzing and absorbing information and charting the course to a new future. As I approached new challenges, I sought to gain perspective by gathering as much information about the historical background as possible and looking for parallels from similar situations in the past. As a pastor, coach and educator I have learned that, while technology has changed through the years, ideas and the dynamics of human relationships have seldom changed. I've also learned that "*there is nothing new under the sun*" (Ecclesiastes 1.9, ESV).

The Context strength allows me to quickly analyze the present by studying the past. As long as I can remember, I had a passion for history. More than just the dates and facts, people and ideas from the past fascinated me. I discovered that I have the innate ability to see the connection between the past and present and how past events shape the trajectory of the future. I could see where I had come from and where I was going. The strengths-based leadership materials likened this process to a car's rearview mirror. While it may seem counterintuitive, I firmly believe that I become wiser about the future as I study the past because I know that its seeds were sown there. In the end I have confidence in my decisions because I know that they are firmly grounded in a historical context.

A Scripture text that comes to mind when I think of the Context theme is Deuteronomy 4.1-10. In this narrative, Moses prepares to give Israel the covenant laws that would set them apart from their neighbors. He does this in the context of their experience of God in history. They know how God will judge disobedience and bless obedience in the future because they have seen how he responded in the past. People may change, but God cannot change and he will remain faithful to his covenant with his people. As the generations who see these things guard their hearts and share what they have seen with future generations, they will pass on a legacy of faithfulness and blessing.

Deliberative

Deliberative Strength Highlight — *People strong in the Deliberative theme are best described by the serious care they take in making decisions or choices. They anticipate the obstacles.*

Scriptural Support for the Deliberative Strength

Luke 14.28-32 — "If one of you is planning to build a tower, you sit down first and figure out what it will cost, to see if you have enough money to finish the job. If you don't, you will not be able to finish the tower after laying the foundation; and all who see what happened will make fun of you. 'You began to build but can't finish the job!' they will say. If a king goes out with ten thousand men to fight another king who comes against him with twenty thousand men, he will sit down first and decide if he is strong enough to face that other king. If he isn't, he will send messengers to meet the other king to ask for terms of peace while he is still a long way off."

Ephesians 5.15, 16 — So be careful how you live. Don't live like ignorant people, but like wise people. Make good use of every opportunity you have, because these are evil days.

James 1.19, 20 — Remember this, my dear friends! Everyone must be quick to listen, but slow to speak and slow to become angry. Human anger does not achieve God's righteous purpose.

Gideon and the Deliberative Strength

Judges 6.33-40 — Then all the Midianites, the Amalekites, and the desert tribes assembled, crossed the Jordan River, and camped in Jezreel Valley. The spirit of the Lord took control of Gideon, and he blew a trumpet to call the men of the clan of Abiezer to follow him. He sent messengers throughout the territory of both parts of Manasseh to call them to follow him. He sent messengers to the tribes of Asher, Zebulun, and Naphtali, and they also came to join him. Then Gideon said to God, "You say that you have decided to use me to rescue Israel. Well, I am putting some wool on the ground where we thresh the wheat. If in the morning there is dew only on the wool but not on the ground, then I will know that you are going to use me to rescue Israel." That is exactly what happened. When Gideon got up early the next morning, he squeezed the wool and wrung enough dew out of it to fill a bowl with water. Then Gideon said to God, "Don't be angry with me; let me speak just once more. Please let me make one more test with the wool. This time let the wool be dry, and the ground be wet." That night God did that very thing. The next morning the wool was dry, but the ground was wet with dew.

Deeper Dive

- What causes Gideon to want to avoid making a poor decision?
- How does his Deliberative strength impact Gideon's interaction with God?
- What are some possible tension points for a Deliberative person who is trusting God today?
- What 'fleece' have you asked of God? How do you help others think through decisions?

Challenge: Whatever your role, take responsibility for helping others think through their decisions.

Appreciation: Encourage someone with the Deliberative strength to take the lead in a situation where caution and the ability to anticipate danger is needed.

ENGAGE YOUR STRENGTHS STORIES

Rubin Crespo—*Chaplain, U.S. Army*

Taking time to consider my options has been my primary approach to making decisions. As early as elementary school, I would do research to show my mom what would be the best value in a bicycle purchase. The "Deliberative" approach to decision making, as I grew older, could be highlighted by the hours that I would spend researching the pros and cons of different summer camps and later the pros and cons of certain colleges. Even the way I approached the sport of wrestling was quite deliberative as I would slowly set up my favorite offensive moves by enticing my opponents to take what I would give them, thus always attempting to maximize the risk to reward ratio. My coach jokingly yelled "coma" as he saw me very slowly set up a roll that I almost always took after I was comfortable with how much control I had of my opponent's arm and leg.

The leaders that had this Deliberative strength could easily be recognized as we utilized the Military Decision Making Process prior to exercises and deployments missions. They were the ever so important personnel that would thoroughly enjoy the process of weeding through the second and third order effects of various courses of action until decisions were made. My transition from Infantry Soldier to Army Chaplain was a very deliberative process that involved considering many of the ways that God had been working in me and through me as I studied, received and shared the love of Christ. As a Battalion Chaplain serving over 800 Soldiers, a deliberative approach to ministry was necessary in order to spend time with Soldiers from each company as often as possible and touch lives in different ways depending upon the needs of each particular Soldier, squad, platoon or company. As Soldiers and families seek direction at some of the most extreme moments of their lives, carefully and compassionately listening to their story helps to sift through their situation to provide perspective and guidance based upon the Word of God.

The directive in Ephesians 5.15-16 (NIV) to "*Be very careful, then, how you live- not as unwise but as wise, making the most of every opportunity, because the days are evil,*" became increasingly important as I became a husband and father. As I prepare to send my youngest son off to college next year, I see how my deliberative analysis of colleges, entry requirements, and scholarships has helped a young man who is anything but deliberative to have an eye opening look at future opportunities. Such a deliberative approach to your walk with God will allow you to avoid the pitfalls of this world and to give thanks to God for everything.

Developer

Developer Strength Highlight – *People strong in the Developer theme recognize and cultivate the potential in others. They spot the signs of each small improvement and derive satisfaction from these improvements.*

Scriptural Support for the Developer Strength

1 Timothy 4.15, 16 — Practice these things and devote yourself to them, in order that your progress may be seen by all. Watch yourself and watch your teaching. Keep on doing these things, because if you do, you will save both yourself and those who hear you.

1 Thessalonians 2.7b-12 — But we were gentle when we were with you, like a mother taking care of her children. Because of our love for you we were ready to share with you not only the Good News from God but even our own lives. You were so dear to us! Surely you remember, our friends, how we worked and toiled! We worked day and night so that we would not be any trouble to you as we preached to you the Good News from God. You are our witnesses, and so is God, that our conduct toward you who believe was pure, right, and without fault. You know that we treated each one of you just as parents treat their own children. We encouraged you, we comforted you, and we kept urging you to live the kind of life that pleases God, who calls you to share in his own Kingdom and glory.

Barnabas – A Developer

Acts 11.22-26 — The news about this reached the church in Jerusalem, so they sent Barnabas to Antioch. When he arrived and saw how God had blessed the people, he was glad and urged them all to be faithful and true to the Lord with all their hearts. Barnabas was a good man, full of the

Holy Spirit and faith, and many people were brought to the Lord. Then Barnabas went to Tarsus to look for Saul. When he found him, he took him to Antioch, and for a whole year the two met with the people of the church and taught a large group. It was at Antioch that the believers were first called Christians.

Acts 15.35-40 — Paul and Barnabas spent some time in Antioch, and together with many others they taught and preached the word of the Lord. Some time later Paul said to Barnabas, "Let us go back and visit the believers in every town where we preached the word of the Lord, and let us find out how they are getting along." Barnabas wanted to take John Mark with them, but Paul did not think it was right to take him, because he had not stayed with them to the end of their mission, but had turned back and left them in Pamphylia. There was a sharp argument, and they separated: Barnabas took Mark and sailed off for Cyprus, while Paul chose Silas and left, commended by the believers to the care of the Lord's grace.

Deeper Dive

- When Barnabas first arrived in Antioch what did he encourage the church to do?
- Why did Barnabas seek out Paul for this essential ministry?
- While preparing for the second missionary journey, what was the disagreement? How was it decided? What do you think Barnabas saw in John Mark?
- What do you see in someone that others may not see in him/her? Name a person who has personally invested in your growth and development.

Challenge: Choose one person and share with them the great potential you see in them.

Appreciation: Ask a Developer to consider several people in your group and explain the hidden potential they see and how they would plan to develop this potential.

ENGAGE YOUR STRENGTHS STORIES

Corie Weathers—*Licensed Professional Counselor, Military Spouse, Speaker and Advocate*

For as long as I can remember, I have been known as "The Encourager." As a young adult, I was always more interested in bringing life out of others than in cheering from the sidelines. My heart for encouraging others eventually led me down the easy path to becoming a professional counselor and later towards recognizing potential in churches, ministries, and organizations. Being a military spouse has provided an opportunity for me to advocate for better resources for military families as well as encourage spouses to thrive in their circumstances rather than survive. As a wife and mother, I believe that being invested in personal growth is essential to the success of a family.

As a counselor, my clients often come in with little to no hope for their situation. Offering my strength as a Developer provides the patience and support they need to grow and reach their full potential and purpose. Whether it is with an individual or organization, I easily get excited about opportunities to help develop a program, break through obstacles that hold back greatness, and take someone or something to the next level. Brainstorming new growth opportunities and helping teams get "unstuck" energizes me and produces a true feeling of accomplishment. My husband says I can see the silver lining in anything, and it's true! My favorite phrase is "everything is grist for the mill" – meaning, we can learn from anything we go through and ultimately be better for it. Learning how to invest in and leverage my Developer strength has propelled me toward my own potential by learning the skills necessary to reach my goals. Frequent moves in the military used to be challenging for me as I would often find myself in a place where I felt I had no one in whom to invest. This has motivated me to learn web design, marketing, and public speaking to inspire growth in others. By expanding my ministry presence online, I am able to continue my ministry, even during transitions.

With talent, comes the responsibility to use it well. I am often reminded in my walk with God that I cannot take ownership for someone else's decision to grow or not grow. I am, however, responsible for making sure that I am growing in my personal walk with God. 1 Timothy 4.15, 16 reminds me that my personal development impacts others, especially my family. When I devote my day, my talents, and my time to the Lord, he creates divine opportunities that lead to success. With holiness as my goal, I can "die to self" and focus on what is most important rather than what the world could ever offer.

Discipline

Discipline Strength Highlight — *People strong in the Discipline theme enjoy routine and structure. Their world is best described by the order they create.*

Scriptural Support for the Discipline Strength

1 Chronicles 28.19 — King David said, "All this is contained in the plan written according to the instructions which the Lord himself gave me to carry out."

Proverbs 21.5 — Plan carefully and you will have plenty; if you act too quickly, you will never have enough.

1 Corinthians 14.40 — Everything must be done in a proper and orderly way.

Discipline and the Ten Commandments

Exodus 20.1-17 — God spoke, and these were his words: "I am the Lord your God who brought you out of Egypt, where you were slaves. Worship no god but me. Do not make for yourselves images of anything in heaven or on earth or in the water under the earth. Do not bow down to any idol or worship it, because I am the Lord your God and I tolerate no rivals. I bring punishment on those who hate me and on their descendants down to the third and fourth generation. But I show my love to thousands of generations of those who love me and obey my laws. Do not use my name for evil purposes, for I, the Lord your God, will punish anyone who misuses my name. Observe the Sabbath and keep it holy. You have six days in which to do your work, but the seventh day is a day of rest dedicated to me. On that day no one is to work — neither you, your children, your slaves, your animals, nor the foreigners who live in your country. In six days I, the Lord, made the earth, the sky, the seas, and everything in them, but on the seventh day I rested. That is why I, the Lord, blessed the Sabbath and made it holy. Respect your father and your mother, so that you may live a long time in the land that I am giving you. Do not commit murder. Do not commit adultery. Do not steal. Do not accuse anyone falsely. Do not desire another man's house; do not desire his wife, his slaves, his cattle, his donkeys, or anything else that he owns."

Deeper Dive

- God spoke and gave us ten commands by which to live. Where else has God spoken and created order?
- Why is it essential to live by the Ten Commandments?
- Is it possible to live within the parameters of these rules and obtain happiness?
- Do you see a progression of values within the commandments? Using this example, how can you create order in your personal life and community?

Challenge: Use your uncanny ability to generate structure to bring order, rest and blessing into the Kingdom mission around you.

Appreciation: Observe and learn from those with tremendous Discipline – but don't let them miss out on new adventures serving God.

ENGAGE YOUR STRENGTHS STORIES

Thomas R. Strong—*Chaplain, U.S. Army*

Many see Discipline as something painful, yet it is the practice in my life which bears fruit. I grew up in a relationally chaotic family and the way I coped was to create order amidst the chaos. It helped me move forward, grow, and mature. Later on I became a U.S. Navy Nuclear Submarine Officer, worked in the engineering sales field for a then Fortune 300 company, and pastored for six years. Currently, I am a U.S. Army Chaplain. One thread that I have noticed through all my experiences is that success is not so much the great things I've done, but rather, "not shooting myself in the foot." This has come about through Discipline, like a Soldier trained to rightly use his weapon. Discipline in my life is something I have used to my advantage to produce the best outcomes and minimize risks.

For many years, I pridefully wavered between thinking I was so much better than others in creating order out of chaos to wishing that I was not so stuck on needing order in my life! Through *Engage Your Strengths*, I discovered that Discipline was a talent and a gift from God to develop and benefit others; I was liberated to become more of who God made me to be. It caused me to walk with more of a humble-confidence. I was humbled knowing it was a gift to be used to build up others. I walked with greater confidence knowing that this is who God made me to be, despite it being one of the five rarest of the thirty-four talents. After we returned from an extra-long, arduous deployment, I remember a Soldier of a non-Christian faith thanking me for being calm in the midst of our life-and -death situations. I now realize that it was my Discipline coupled with faith.

Some say that the Holy Spirit works in the moment and thus they do not focus much on planning. From my perspective, I see him working in the moment and also as much, if not more, in the planning and preparation. In response to chaos in the church, the apostle Paul says in 1 Corinthians 14.40 (NIV), "*But everything should be done in a fitting and orderly way.*" I like to plan and develop progress in all areas of my life. My biggest challenge related to Discipline is to remember Proverbs 16.9, "*In his heart a man plans his course, but the Lord determines his steps.*" It's good to plan, but then we must allow God to own the plans so that his will is done.

Empathy

Empathy Strength Highlight — *People strong in the Empathy theme can sense the feelings of other people by imagining themselves in others' lives or others' situations.*

Scriptural Support for the Empathy Strength

2 Kings 20.4-6 — Isaiah left the king, but before he had passed through the central courtyard of the palace the Lord told him to go back to Hezekiah, ruler of the Lord's people, and say to him, "I, the Lord, the God of your ancestor David, have heard your prayer and seen your tears. I will heal you, and in three days you will go to the Temple. I will let you live fifteen years longer. I will rescue you and this city Jerusalem from the emperor of Assyria. I will defend this city, for the sake of my own honor and because of the promise I made to my servant David."

Romans 12.15 — Be happy with those who are happy, weep with those who weep.

Jesus Demonstrating Empathy Over Lazarus

John 11.17-44 — When Jesus arrived, he found that Lazarus had been buried four days before. Bethany was less than two miles from Jerusalem, and many Judeans had come to see Martha and Mary to comfort them about their brother's death. When Martha heard that Jesus was coming, she went out to meet him, but Mary stayed in the house. Martha said to Jesus, "If you had been here, Lord, my brother would not have died! But I know that even now God will give you whatever you ask him for." "Your brother will rise to life," Jesus told her. "I know," she replied, "that he will rise to life on the last day." Jesus said to her, "I am the resurrection and the life. Those who believe in me will live, even though they die; and those who live and believe in me will never die. Do you believe this?" "Yes, Lord!" she answered. "I do believe that you are the Messiah, the Son of God, who was to come into the world." After Martha said this, she went back and called her sister Mary privately. "The Teacher is here," she told her, "and is asking for you." When Mary heard this, she got up and hurried out to meet him (Jesus had not yet arrived in the village, but was still in the place where Martha had met him.) The people who were in the house with Mary comforting her followed her when they saw her get up and hurry out. They thought that she was going to the grave to weep there. Mary arrived where Jesus was, and as soon as she saw him, she fell at his feet. "Lord," she said, "if you had been here, my brother would not have died!" Jesus saw her weeping, and he saw how the people with her were weeping also; his heart was touched, and he was deeply moved. "Where have you buried him?" he asked them. "Come and see, Lord," they answered. Jesus wept. "See how much he loved him!" the people said. But some of them said, "He gave sight to the blind man, didn't he? Could he not have kept Lazarus from dying?" Deeply moved once more, Jesus went to the tomb, which was a cave with a stone placed at the entrance. "Take the stone away!" Jesus ordered. Martha, the dead man's sister, answered, "There will be a bad smell, Lord. He has been buried four days!" Jesus said to her, "Didn't I tell you that you would see God's glory if you believed?" They took the stone away. Jesus looked up and said, "I thank you, Father, that you listen to me. I know that you always listen to me, but I say this for the sake of the people here, so that they will believe that you sent me." After he had said this, he called out in a loud voice, "Lazarus, come out!" He came out, his hands and feet wrapped in grave cloths, and with a cloth around his face. "Untie him," Jesus told them, "and let him go."

Deeper Dive

- Who does Jesus meet first when he arrives in Bethany? What is their discussion about?
- Who does Jesus meet next when he arrives in Bethany? How is this encounter different from the first one?
- What is Jesus' reaction to these encounters? How does he respond?
- Name a time when someone accurately knew how you felt and responded in a helpful way. What can you do to help a person who is in emotional pain?

Challenge: Communicate to others how you perceive the emotional state of people and groups.

Appreciation: Consult someone with Empathy to better understand how a person is feeling about a situation or event and the best way to respond.

ENGAGE YOUR STRENGTHS STORIES

Jeri Strong—*Army Wife, Licensed Professional Counselor Intern*

I recently completed my degree in counseling and am pursuing licensure as a Professional Counselor. I have always had a keen sense of other people's emotional state, as well as the emotional tone of gatherings of people. However, growing up in a home that did not value emotional intelligence, I found it difficult to regulate and manage strong emotions. Years later, I learned that I have the strength of Empathy, and as I developed it, my emotional life made much better sense. I often feel the highs and lows of life to a greater degree than others. Many years ago, I took my first counseling class and started to understand and utilize this great gift of valuing all aspects of our emotional existence. This led me to helping others understand and celebrate this wonderful aspect of being human.

The Empathy strength enables me to have great compassion for other people. Understanding what others may feel helps me to put myself in their shoes. I am often asked by my husband, children, and friends to give my perspective on various situations. Empathy allows me to help them put words to what they are experiencing, which then allows them to figure out what their next steps. In my role as a therapist, I am able to use Empathy to help clients discern what they are really feeling inside. They are then able to verbalize, discern and integrate these feelings, bringing clarity and congruence. As I help couples access and express their underlying feelings to each other, I enable them to emotionally connect. Many have affirmed that my relationships have emotional depth and my discerning feedback provides them with unique insight and perspective.

Our Lord Jesus was a man of great compassion, as recorded in John 11.17-44. Jesus' heart was touched and he was deeply moved, not once but twice, upon seeing Mary and others weeping in response to Lazarus' death. I, too, am often moved to compassion when I see others in pain. As Jesus shows us, tears are the appropriate response to tears. Romans 12.15 explicitly instructs us to mirror our responses to others' expressions, "*Be happy with those who are happy, weep with those who weep.*" Being present with others in all of life's events, and the resulting emotions, is something that I truly enjoy and embrace. I often ask myself when interacting with others, "How can I show care, concern, and understanding to this person?"

Focus

Focus Strength Highlight – *People strong in the Focus theme can take a direction, follow through, and make the corrections necessary to stay on track. They prioritize, then act.*

Scriptural Support for the Focus Strength

Luke 9.51 — As the time drew near when Jesus would be taken up to heaven, he made up his mind and set out on his way to Jerusalem.

Hebrews 12.1,2 — As for us, we have this large crowd of witnesses around us. So then, let us rid ourselves of everything that gets in the way, and of the sin which holds on to us so tightly, and let us run with determination the race that lies before us. Let us keep our eyes fixed on Jesus, on whom our faith depends from beginning to end. He did not give up because of the cross! On the contrary, because of the joy that was waiting for him, he thought nothing of the disgrace of dying on the cross, and he is now seated at the right side of God's throne.

Paul Keeps his Focus

Philippians 3.9b-20 — I now have the righteousness that is given through faith in Christ, the righteousness that comes from God and is based on faith. All I want is to know Christ and to experience the power of his resurrection, to share in his sufferings and become like him in his death, in the hope that I myself will be raised from death to life. I do not claim that I have already succeeded or have already become perfect. I keep striving to win the prize for which Christ Jesus has already won me to himself. Of course, my friends, I really do not think that I have already won it; the one thing I do, however, is to forget what is behind me and do my best to reach what is ahead. So I run straight toward the goal in order to win the prize, which is God's call through Christ Jesus to the life above. All of us who are spiritually mature should have this same attitude. But if some of you have a different attitude, God will make this clear to you. However that may be, let us go forward according to the same rules we have followed until now. Keep on imitating me, my friends. Pay attention to those who follow the right example that we have set for you. I have told you this many times before, and now I repeat it with tears: there are many whose lives make them enemies of Christ's death on the cross. They are going to end up in hell, because their god is their bodily desires. They are proud of what they should be ashamed of, and they think only of things that belong to this world. We, however, are citizens of heaven, and we eagerly wait for our Savior, the Lord Jesus Christ, to come from heaven.

Deeper Dive

- Why do you think Paul uses athletic imagery to illustrate our need to focus on Christ? What other images could he have used to make his point?
- Do you think Paul was able to consistently forget what was behind in order to reach what was ahead?
- Has your Focus talent ever forced you to filter and instinctively evaluate whether or not a particular action will help you move forward toward your goal? If so, describe the situation.
- How often do you begin with the end in mind?

Challenge: Seek clarity through concentration and direction to persevere.

Appreciation: Encourage leaders with the Focus talent to evaluate and determine priorities and to get on course quickly.

ENGAGE YOUR STRENGTHS STORIES

Rob Smith—*Senior Philanthropic Advisor*

During my early life, I recall being focused on goals even before I knew definition of goals. If I needed to accomplish even a short-term goal, I was determined to continue working at it until the task was finished. At times, when I am completely focused on a goal, I almost lose track of time and other activities, but I usually get that task completed. My family admires and appreciates the fact that I keep "first things first," by making important decisions, in light of my faith in God and the needs of my family. Although I function somewhat methodically, I make decisions based on the highest priorities in my life. Then, I am able to develop a plan of action and follow through to complete the most important goals.

My Focus talent helps me to prioritize and then take action. It helps me to set goals. These goals serve as a compass, helping me to determine priorities and make alterations, when needed, to get back on course. I find Focus to be powerful because it forces me to filter and evaluate each action before carrying it out to determine whether it will help me reach my goal. In the end, my Focus talent pushes me to be efficient. By knowing the leads I should pursue, I am better able to raise funds. While others may often start to wander down divergent avenues, I am able to stay on the main road investing in relationship with people who are Kingdom-minded. I am also able to help my team members avoid time-consuming distractions and keep our team on point.

I love how the apostle Paul keeps his Focus in Philippians 3.13-14 "*I really do not think that I have already won it; the one thing I do, however, is to forget what is behind me and do my best to reach what is ahead. So*

I run straight toward the goal in order to win the prize, which is God's call through Christ Jesus to the life above." In my world, understanding that it is not simply about focus, but Godly-focus, is crucial. I ask the Lord to remind me to be intensely and intentionally single-minded towards the things of his Kingdom. That is why Hebrews 12.2 is also an important guide in my life, "*Let us keep our eyes fixed on Jesus, on whom our faith depends from beginning to end.*"

Futuristic

Futuristic Strength Highlight – *People strong in the Futuristic theme are inspired by the future and what could be. They inspire others with their visions of the future.*

Scriptural Support for the Futuristic Strength

Jeremiah 29.11 —I alone know the plans I have for you, plans to bring you prosperity and not disaster, plans to bring about the future you hope for.

Joel 2.28 — Afterward I will pour out my Spirit on everyone: your sons and daughters will proclaim my message; your old people will have dreams, and your young people will see visions.

Matthew 26.64 — Jesus answered him, "So you say. But I tell all of you: from this time on you will see the Son of Man sitting at the right side of the Almighty and coming on the clouds of heaven!"

Hebrews 11.16 — Instead, it was a better country they longed for, the heavenly country. And so God is not ashamed for them to call him their God, because he has prepared a city for them.

Joseph the Futurist

Genesis 37.5-8 — One time Joseph had a dream, and when he told his brothers about it, they hated him even more. He said, "Listen to the dream I had. We were all in the field tying up sheaves of wheat, when my sheaf got up and stood up straight. Yours formed a circle around mine and bowed down to it." "Do you think you are going to be a king and rule over us?" his brothers asked. So they hated him even more because of his dreams and because of what he said about them. Then Joseph had another dream and told his brothers, "I had another dream, in which I saw the sun, the moon, and eleven stars bowing down to me." He also told the dream to his father, and his father scolded him: "What kind of a dream is that? Do you think that your mother, your brothers, and I are going to come and bow down to you?" Joseph's brothers were jealous of him, but his father kept thinking about the whole matter.

Deeper Dive

- How well defined are Joseph's dreams? Do his brothers and father completely understand them?
- How can Joseph's dream be better understood and more easily received?
- Describe a dream that you have for the future.
- How clearly and precisely defined is your dream?

Challenge: Use great wisdom and discernment to communicate your dream/vision to others. They may not see things as clearly as you do.

Appreciation: Help a Futurist to describe the dream/vision more clearly by asking questions and offering your understanding of the vision.

ENGAGE YOUR STRENGTHS STORIES

Tommy "Urban D." Kyllonen—*Lead Pastor, Author, Hip-Hop Artist*

I grew up in a lower income home as my father pastored a church in Philadelphia. This created a work ethic in me from a young age. If I wanted to buy something I had to work for it. I shoveled snow, raked leaves, laid carpet, and cleaned offices, just to name a few of my odd jobs. This helped to develop my ability to always look beyond where

I was at the time, and dream and plan concerning where I could be. Even as a kid, in order to build a fort, I'd round up my neighborhood friends and we'd build it. These small feats in my early years helped shape me to dream, build and accomplish much larger things for God's Kingdom.

The Futuristic strength allows me to see what could be and what should be. I've been in full-time urban ministry for nearly 20 years, and the needs in the urban community are overwhelming. Many people in the community are paralyzed in their brokenness and don't see much of a future. Many people outside of the community look at all the brokenness and don't envision any future. God has helped me to not only identify the needs, but also create solutions. As the lead pastor of Crossover Church, God has used me to lead our church from a handful of people with no vision to a church of over a thousand that oozes with vision for our people and our city.

When you see the future, some people think you are crazy. You look at things with possibility and hope, where others see impossibility and hopelessness. This has been much of my story doing urban ministry in the trenches. But, with each victory, my strength becomes stronger and I'm encouraged even more that I'm born for this and that God will provide the provision for the vision. I often lean on the story of Joseph, the Futurist, in Genesis 37.5-8. Another passage that has become an anthem for me is Ephesians 3.0. It talks about God being able to accomplish more than we could ever dream or ask. This is what wakes me up every morning. I'm excited to create, cultivate, and complete some new accomplishments for God's glory!

Harmony

Harmony Strength Highlight – *People strong in the Harmony theme look for consensus. They don't enjoy conflict; rather they seek areas of agreement.*

Scriptural Support for the Harmony Strength

Romans 12.16-18 — Have the same concern for everyone. Do not be proud, but accept humble duties. Do not think of yourselves as wise. If someone has done you wrong, do not repay him with a wrong. Try to do what everyone considers to be good. Do everything possible on your part to live in peace with everybody.

1 Corinthians 1.10 — By the authority of our Lord Jesus Christ I appeal to all of you, my friends, to agree in what you say, so that there will be no divisions among you. Be completely united, with only one thought and one purpose.

Philippians 2.1-5 — Your life in Christ makes you strong, and his love comforts you. You have fellowship with the Spirit, and you have kindness and compassion for one another. I urge you, then, to make me completely happy by having the same thoughts, sharing the same love, and being one in soul and mind. Don't do anything from selfish ambition or from a cheap desire to boast, but be humble toward one another, always considering others better than yourselves. And look out for one another's interests, not just for your own. The attitude you should have is the one that Christ Jesus had.

Abram and Lot Choose Harmony

Genesis 13.8-18 — Then Abram said to Lot, "We are relatives, and your men and my men shouldn't be quarreling. So let's separate. Choose any part of the land you want. You go one way, and I'll go the other." Lot looked around and saw that the whole Jordan Valley, all the way to Zoar, had plenty of water, like the Garden of the Lord or like the land of Egypt. (This was before the Lord had destroyed the cities of Sodom and Gomorrah.) So Lot chose the whole Jordan Valley for himself and moved away toward the east. That is how the two men parted. Abram stayed in the land of Canaan, and Lot settled among the cities in the valley and camped near Sodom, whose people were wicked and sinned against the Lord. After Lot had left, the Lord said to Abram, "From where you are, look carefully in all directions. I am going to give you and your descendants all the land that you see, and it will be yours forever. *I am going to give you so many descendants that no one will be able to count them all; it would be as easy to count all the specks of dust on earth!* Now, go and look over the whole land, because I am going to give it all to you." So Abram moved his camp and settled near the sacred trees of Mamre at Hebron, and there he built an altar tothe Lord.

Deeper Dive

- How does Abram's willingness to sacrifice his personal gain defuse a potential conflict?
- How are humility and peace-making related in this passage?
- How does Abram's Harmony strength change his relationship with Lot?
- In what ways does seeking consensus strengthen your group for future opportunities?

Challenge: Use your ability to find common ground to create harmony in your team.

Appreciation: Encourage a team member with the Harmony strength not to simply run away from conflict, but to use his or her consensus building skills to resolve conflict without confrontation.

ENGAGE YOUR STRENGTHS STORIES

Jennifer Cook—*U.S. Army Chaplain's Wife, PWOC Leader*

Being raised in a family of six children, encountering conflict and finding resolution started at a very young age. I realized early on that I had a desire to keep my environment peaceful, oftentimes going along with the flow for unity's sake. Now, being married to an Army Chaplain, I realize that my role affords me a great opportunity to make an impact on the emotional well-being of women around me. This truly gives me excitement as I find myself in the lives of women who are searching, seeking, and longing for peace in their hearts.

Through *Engage Your Strengths*, I realized that my natural strength is Harmony. Almost daily, I find myself in conversations encouraging women to find resolution amidst the struggles they walk through. As a Christian, I see the greatest hope in finding that resolution is in imitating the calm and even-keeled example we had in Christ, as he led men and women down a road of finding inner peace and harmony. Women are complex characters, and oftentimes, come with bags trailing behind us. My desire is always to seek the practical, down-to-earth solutions and help others process them without wasting emotional energy on the situation. Also, bringing women together through Bible studies and fellowship energizes me to use this strength, as we focus on areas such as marriage or spiritual growth. We come together in outward unity.

We grow together with inner unity.

I am reminded of the story of Abram and Lot, whose herders were quarreling, finding it difficult to live in the same land together. Abram knew this could not continue, and sought a peaceful solution in allowing Lot to choose any part of the land. Abram's wisdom brought harmony to his own people as Lot moved away toward Sodom and the east. The negative effects of the friction were now gone, leaving room for Abram's people to live in peace and grow according to the LORD's promise recorded in Genesis 13.16 – "*I am going to give you so many descendants that no one will be able to count them all; it would be as easy to count all the specks of dust on earth!*" By allowing harmony to prevail, the land was open to grow! By allowing harmony to prevail in our hearts, our lives are more open to grow…deeper… and wider… beyond what we can imagine!

Ideation

> **Ideation Strength Highlight** – *People strong in the Ideation theme are fascinated by ideas. They are able to find connections between seemingly disparate phenomena.*

Scriptural Support for the Ideation Strength

Isaiah 43.19 — Watch for the new thing I am going to do. It is happening already — you can see it now! I will make a road through the wilderness and give you streams of water there.

Isaiah 65.17, 18 — The Lord says, "I am making a new earth and new heavens. The events of the past will be completely forgotten. Be glad and rejoice forever in what I create. The new Jerusalem I make will be full of joy, and her people will be happy."

Romans 12.2 — Do not conform yourselves to the standards of this world, but let God transform you inwardly by a complete change of your mind. Then you will be able to know the will of God — what is good and is pleasing to him and is perfect.

Think of Excellence

Philippians 4.1-9 — So then, my friends, how dear you are to me and how I miss you! How happy you make me, and how proud I am of you! This, dear friends, is how you should stand firm in your life in the Lord. Euodia and Syntyche, please, I beg you, try to agree as sisters in the Lord. And you too, my faithful partner, I want you to help these women; for they have worked hard with me to spread the gospel, together with Clement and all my other fellow workers, whose names are in God's book of the living. May you always be joyful in your union with the Lord. I say it again: rejoice!

Show a gentle attitude toward everyone. The Lord is coming soon. Don't worry about anything, but in all your prayers ask God for what you need, always asking him with a thankful heart. And God's peace, which is far beyond human understanding, will keep your hearts and minds safe in union with Christ Jesus. In conclusion, my friends, fill your minds with those things that are good and that deserve praise: things that are true, noble, right, pure, lovely, and honorable. Put into practice what you learned and received from me, both from my words and from my actions. And the God who gives us peace will be with you.

Deeper Dive

- How does Paul encourage the Philippians?
- What instructions does Paul give to the Philippians?
- With what concepts or ideas does Paul encourage the Philippians to fill their minds?
- With what concepts or ideas should you fill your mind in order to please the Lord and bring peace?

Challenge: Explain to others how you see connections that undergird unifying concepts.

Appreciation: Encourage a person with Ideation to examine a complex situation or problem, then ask them to list a number of creative and/or unique possible solutions.

ENGAGE YOUR STRENGTHS STORIES

Brian Shore—*Pastor, Educator, Leadership Coach*

A few years ago, I was part of a team that planted a church in South Florida. After working with each other for a while, and before we discovered Strengths vocabulary, we described each other as characters from Winnie the Pooh. The worship leader was Pooh, the CFO was Eyor, and I was Tigger. I hope that I was called Tigger because I was energetic, creative, and always bubbling with new ideas. In my life as a husband, father, grandfather, pastor, professor, coach, and consultant people are constantly engaging me in conversation and looking for new ideas. As a follower of Christ, it excites me to collaborate with others, sharing ideas and growing together.

The Ideation strength allows me to think creatively. For my friends who are concrete, linear thinkers, I describe this process as "sand thinking." "Sand thinking" is malleable and flowing. It is fresh and allows me to think without constraints or limitations. Often, while thinking like this, especially in collaboration with others, we come up with a really new idea. Do you see the image? Thinking in the sandbox of thought, moving words and sentences around, building sandcastles of hope. It's fun, exciting, risky, and productive.

In Romans Chapter 2, the apostle Paul compels us to be transformed by the renewing of our minds. As followers of Christ, Paul, in Second Corinthians, describes us as new creations. We were once dead in our trespasses and sins, but are now alive to God. Part of this renewal is the reshaping of our thoughts and ideas. The Ideation strength came alive for me when I became a follower of Christ. As I thought about those things that are true, right, pure, lovely, and honorable, and put those things into practice, I was free to think, dream, and create without constraint. Philippians 4 has a powerful impact on my life. Occasionally, others who have different strengths describe me as a dreamer or say that I'm impractical. That's ok because as we work together they often, eventually, see the fruit of my idea and then say "Oh, I get it now!" They help bring my idea into reality and so we go from the sandbox of ideas to concrete dreams realized.

Includer

Includer Strength Highlight — *People strong in the Includer theme are accepting of others. They show awareness of those who feel left out, and make an effort to include them.*

Scriptural Support for the Includer Strength

John 3.16 — For God loved the world so much that he gave his only Son, so that everyone who believes in him may not die but have eternal life.

Romans 15.7 — Accept one another, then, for the glory of God, as Christ has accepted you.

Ephesians 2.13 — But now, in union with Christ Jesus you, who used to be far away, have been brought near by the blood of Christ.

Acts 10.34, 35 — Peter began to speak: "I now realize that it is true that God treats everyone on the same basis. Those who fear him and do what is right are acceptable to him, no matter what race they belong to."

Includer in Ruth

Ruth 2.11-23 — Boaz answered, "I have heard about everything that you have done for your mother-in-law since your husband died. I know how you left your father and mother and your own country and how you came to live among a people you had never known before. May the Lord reward you for what you have done. May you have a full reward from the Lord God of Israel, to whom you have come for protection!" Ruth answered, "You are very kind to me, sir. You have made me feel better by speaking gently to me, even though I am not the equal of one of your servants." At mealtime Boaz said to Ruth, "Come and have a piece of bread, and dip it in the sauce." So she sat with the workers, and Boaz passed some roasted grain to her. She ate until she was satisfied, and she still had some food left over. After she had left to go and gather grain, Boaz ordered the workers, "Let her gather grain even where the bundles are lying, and don't say anything to stop her. Besides that, pull out some heads of grain from the bundles and leave them for her to pick up." So Ruth gathered grain in the field until evening, and when she had beaten it out, she found she had nearly twenty-five pounds. She took the grain back into town and showed her mother-in-law how much she had gathered. She also gave her the food left over from the meal. Naomi asked her, "Where did you gather all this grain today? Whose field have you been working in? May God bless the man who took an interest in you!" So Ruth told Naomi that she had been working in a field belonging to a man named Boaz. "May the Lord bless Boaz!" Naomi exclaimed. "The Lord always keeps his promises to the living and the dead." And she went on, "That man is a close relative of ours, one of those responsible for taking care of us." Then Ruth said, "Best of all, he told me to keep gathering grain with his workers until they finish the harvest." Naomi said to Ruth, "Yes, daughter, it will be better for you to work with the women in Boaz' field. You might be molested if you went to someone else's field." So Ruth worked with them and gathered grain until all the barley and wheat had been harvested. And she continued to live with her mother-in-law.

Deeper Dive

- What does Boaz do in order to include and provide for Ruth? Why does he do it?
- What elements of this story foreshadow God's provision for his people through Jesus Christ?

- When people intercede for each other and call upon the name of the Lord, what does that do to the group dynamic?
- How can you better invite those who are outside the group to participate inside the group?

Challenge: Speak up for those who are on the outskirts of the group. Use your gift of inclusion to bring equality to those around you.

Appreciation: Encourage someone with Includer to leverage this ability to strengthen and build up the entire Church body.

ENGAGE YOUR STRENGTHS STORIES

Lisa Northway—*Chaplain, U.S. Army*

From an early age I could articulate the concepts of exclusion and inclusion. I sensed profound loss or great gain depending on how I perceived one's exclusion from or one's inclusion into a particular situation. I remember sitting in my first grade classroom when a school administrator came to lead a boy out of our class forever. Our teacher announced matter-of-factly, and in a somewhat forced cheery voice, that our fellow student was going to the *special* class. Somehow I understood, at that young age, needing to go to the *special* class was not good. There was no time for a proper farewell. He was gone for worse, not better, The next time we caught a glimpse of our former classmate, he was in the kindergarten building, where we were altogether the year before. That couldn't possibly be good, I surmised. Our relationship with this student, as a part of our class, was changed forever.

The *Engage Your Strengths* assessment helps demonstrate how my Includer strength empowers me to be a change agent in my world. Life is about relationships. Broken relationships or a non-relationship status, of some sort, generally calls out in me the desire to facilitate creative conflict resolution. I have come to understand that the driving force of connecting or reconnecting people with each other can ultimately change the destiny of each person to be greater than each one could be on his or her own. I believe our relationships are made more satisfying when we make room for the diversity of passions and talents in each other. My most repeated words to live by for myself and others are: "Make room for a miracle."

In Ruth 2.11-23, Boaz made room for a miracle in his own heart when he considered an unlikely woman; a foreigner and widow, with a remarkable story of courage and self-sacrifice regarding the care of her mother-in-law. His wealth and status in his community easily could have precluded him taking the time to care for a recent immigrant to his country. Boaz understood Ruth had value all her own that deserved recognition in a world that did not naturally make room for her contributions. By accepting Ruth into his community, his home and his heart, Boaz changed both Ruth and Naomi's anticipated outcome and ultimately changed the destiny of their future generations. A complicated and socially marginalized woman was given the benefit of being a full-fledged member of her new community, impacting her quality of life as well as those with whom she shared a life in her new country. Our acceptance of others can lead to a greater understanding of God's acceptance of us when we allow for the miracle of inviting each other into our own communities, homes, and hearts.

Individualization

Individualization Strength Highlight — *People strong in the Individualization theme are intrigued with the unique qualities of each person. They have a gift for figuring out how people who are different can work together productively.*

Scriptural Support for the Individualization Strength

1 Samuel 16.7 — But the Lord said to him, "Pay no attention to how tall and handsome he is. I have rejected him, because I do not judge as people judge. They look at the outward appearance, but I look at the heart."

Matthew 10.1-5a — Jesus called his twelve disciples together and gave them authority to drive out evil spirits and to heal every disease and every sickness. These are the names of the twelve apostles: first, Simon (called Peter) and his brother Andrew; James and his brother John, the sons of Zebedee; Philip and Bartholomew; Thomas and Matthew, the tax collector; James son of Alphaeus, and Thaddaeus; Simon the Patriot, and Judas Iscariot, who betrayed Jesus. These twelve men were sent out by Jesus.

1 Corinthians 12.12, 28 — Christ is like a single body, which has many parts; it is still one body, even though it is made up of different parts . . . . In the church God has put all in place: in the first place apostles, in the second place prophets, and in the third place teachers; then those who perform miracles, followed by those who are given the power to heal or to help others or to direct them or to speak in strange tongues.

Moses and the Strength of Individualization

Exodus 35.30-36.1 — Moses said to the Israelites, "The Lord has chosen Bezalel, the son of Uri and grandson of Hur from the tribe of Judah. God has filled him with his power and given him skill, ability, and understanding for every kind of artistic work, for planning skillful designs and working them in gold, silver, and bronze; for cutting jewels to be set; for carving wood; and for every other kind of artistic work. The Lord has given to him and to Oholiab son of Ahisamach, from the tribe of Dan, the ability to teach their crafts to others. He has given them skill in all kinds of work done by engravers, designers, and weavers of fine linen; blue, purple, and red wool; and other cloth. They are able to do all kinds of work and are skillful designers. "Bezalel, Oholiab, and all the other workers to whom the Lord has given skill and understanding, who know how to make everything needed to build the sacred Tent, are to make everything just as the Lord has commanded."

Deeper Dive

- Why did God choose Bezalel and Oholiab to build the sacred tent?
- Where did their unique abilities originate?
- What unique skills did Bezalel and Oholiab have?
- What unique skills has God given you? Share a time when you felt that you were doing what you were made to do.

Challenge: Use your Individualization strength to help put the right person in the right job.

Appreciation: Consult someone with Individualization when preparing to make personnel decisions.

ENGAGE YOUR STRENGTHS STORIES

Mark Forshaw—*Executive Director, Global Scripture Impact*

My hometown of Liverpool, England, is a port city with a rich history. It is an international crossroads with a long-standing cultural mix. I am sure that this culture prepared me to answer God's call and look beyond the borders of the U.K. to first serve as a missionary in East Africa and to then move into international development – ultimately, taking me to more than 25 countries in my work. This has included time with the World Health Organization in Geneva, Switzerland, and subsequently bringing these experiences to serve with American Bible Society, especially as we partner with sister Bible Societies across the globe. Along this exciting journey, I found an Australian wife with whom I had a daughter born in London and a son born in France.

The strength of Individualization has proven to be a significant asset in my journey of work, family, church leader, and kids soccer coach! With a commitment to the existing and potential power that God has placed within local churches and communities, I have sought to identify not so much the *what* that could be done to make a positive change, but *who* can bring about that positive change. What are the latent personal resources that individuals can bring that have been waiting to be released to make a change for good? Whether that be a church-based HIV/AIDS assistance group in India or a U.S. suburban youth soccer team, I am excited when I have the opportunity to assist an individual to identify their skills, the value of their personal experience, and the potential of a new role in a team, church or community that, when combined rightly with others, produces greater things.

I have come to realize that the strength of Individualization, like any other strength, should never be left on the shelf following the initial development of a new team, strategy or plan. Rather, it needs to be used daily to see who God has placed around you that needs encouragement to grow, or to be an asset to a team that needs them to succeed. A team does not succeed by only having an accomplished leader or even a goal scorer. Rather, all the places need to be filled and, above all, valued for their role, then their world can change. As 1 Corinthians 12.12 says, "*Christ is like a single body, which has many parts; it is still one body, even though it is made up of different parts.*" A body that is complete and healthy is one that functions effectively for the purposes set before it. It is a privilege to be part of that body of change.

Input

> **Input Strength Highlight** – *People strong in the Input theme have a craving to know more. They often like to collect and archive all kinds of information.*

Scriptural Support for the Input Strength

Proverbs 2.1-6 — My child, learn what I teach you and never forget what I tell you to do. Listen to what is wise and try to understand it. Yes, beg for knowledge; plead for insight. Look for it as hard as you would for silver or some hidden treasure. If you do, you will know what it means to fear the Lord and you will succeed in learning about God. It is the Lord who gives wisdom; from him come knowledge and understanding.

John 21.25 — Now, there are many other things that Jesus did. If they were all written down one by one, I suppose that the whole world could not hold the books that would be written.

2 Timothy 4.13 — When you come, bring my coat that I left in Troas with Carpus; bring the books too, and especially the ones made of parchment.

Ezra and Input Strength

Ezra 7.1-10 — Many years later, when Artaxerxes was emperor of Persia, there was a man named Ezra. He traced his ancestors back to Aaron, the High Priest, as follows: Ezra was the son of Seraiah, son of Azariah, son of Hilkiah, son of Shallum, son of Zadok, son of Ahitub, son of Amariah, son of Azariah, son of Meraioth, son of Zerahiah, son of Uzzi, son of Bukki, son of Abishua, son of Phinehas, son of Eleazar, son of Aaron. Ezra was a scholar with a thorough knowledge of the Law which the Lord, the God of Israel, had given to Moses. Because Ezra had the blessing of the Lord his

God, the emperor gave him everything he asked for. In the seventh year of the reign of Artaxerxes, Ezra set out from Babylonia for Jerusalem with a group of Israelites which included priests, Levites, Temple musicians, Temple guards, and workers. They left Babylonia on the first day of the first month, and with God's help they arrived in Jerusalem on the first day of the fifth month. Ezra had devoted his life to studying the Law of the Lord, to practicing it, and to teaching all its laws and regulations to the people of Israel.

Deeper Dive

- What do you think Ezra thought when he found the people living contrary to God's Law? How do you believe he felt?
- Why do you think Ezra craved to know more about God and the Law?
- Does your Input talent cause you to collect information that could be helpful to others? If so, describe them.
- How often do you get to provide relevant and tangible help?

Challenge: Be a resource collector for people in your group.

Appreciation: Encourage leaders with Input talent to collect ideas, books, memorabilia, quotations, and facts to facilitate growth wand performance.

ENGAGE YOUR STRENGTHS STORIES

Roderick Mills—*Chaplain, U.S. Army*

All of my life, I've had a voracious passion to cultivate, equip, teach, and inspire others. As a father to five grown children, a church-planter of churches in the U.S. and overseas, and a U.S. Army Chaplain, I have invested in others so they could live their God-given dreams and destiny. I have always viewed my family as my primary discipleship responsibility and as a microcosm of leader development. With four of my five top strengths being in the strategic domain, I have been most comfortable as the consummate student, teacher, and scholar, pursuing and sharing wisdom, knowledge and understanding.

The Input strength has enabled me to enjoyably capture, catalogue, and share my learning with my grown children and their families. By the age of 23, I had three full-size filing cabinets filled with personal studies and teachings, filed by topic. Since the invention of cloud drive technology, I have been able to digitally scan thousands of pages of notes and studies by topic and upload them to the cloud drive. I have also uploaded thousands of my digital study notes and personal journal notes. Every day, I add notes to my Bible through Logos Software, then export them every few months to the shared drive in the cloud. All of my notes and highlights on all my Kindle books are exported to the shared drive as well. Today, my grown children and their families regularly access thousands of pages of my studies, and dozens of audio files of my teachings through the cloud shared drive even though they all live thousands of miles away.

In Proverbs 2.1-6 Solomon instructed his son saying, "*My child, learn what I teach you and never forget what I tell you to do. Listen to what is wise and try to understand it. Yes, beg for knowledge; plead for insight. Look for it as hard as you would for silver or some hidden treasure. If you do, you will know what it means to fear the* L*ORD* *and you will succeed in learning about God. It is the* L*ORD* *who gives wisdom; from him come knowledge and understanding.*" It is a great joy to leave my children a legacy of wisdom and knowledge that's easily accessible to them. In so doing, I am able to inspire and empower them daily to live and impart Solomon's challenge.

Intellection

Intellection Strength Highlight — *People strong in the Intellection theme are characterized by their intellectual activity. They are introspective and appreciate intellectual discussions.*

Scriptural Support for the Intellection Strength

Luke 2.17-19 — When the shepherds saw him, they told them what the angel had said about the child. All who heard it were amazed at what the shepherds said. Mary remembered all these things and thought deeply about them.

Luke 2.46, 47 — On the third day they found him in the Temple, sitting with the Jewish teachers, listening to them and asking questions. All who heard him were amazed at his intelligent answers.

Peter Encourages Intellection

1 Peter 1.13 — So then, have your minds ready for action. Keep alert and set your hope completely on the blessing which will be given you when Jesus Christ is revealed.

Intellection on Mars Hill

Acts 17.16-33 — While Paul was waiting in Athens for Silas and Timothy, he was greatly upset when he noticed how full of idols the city was. So he held discussions in the synagogue with the Jews and with the Gentiles who worshiped God, and also in the public square every day with the people who happened to come by. Certain Epicurean and Stoic teachers also debated with him. Some of them asked, "What is this ignorant show-off trying to say?" Others answered, "He seems to be talking about foreign gods." They said this because Paul was preaching about Jesus and the resurrection. So they took Paul, brought him before the city council, the Areopagus, and said, "We would like to know what this new teaching is that you are talking about. Some of the things we hear you say sound strange to us, and we would like to know what they mean." (For all the citizens of Athens and the foreigners who lived there liked to spend all their time telling and hearing the latest new thing.) Paul stood up in front of the city council and said, "I see that in every way you Athenians are very religious. For as I walked through your city and looked at the places where you worship, I found an altar on which is written, 'To an Unknown God.' That which you worship, then, even though you do not know it, is what I now proclaim to you. God, who made the world and everything in it, is Lord of heaven and earth and does not live in temples made by human hands. Nor does he need anything that we can supply by working for him, since it is he himself who gives life and breath and everything else to everyone. From one human being he created all races of people and made them live throughout the whole earth. He himself fixed beforehand the exact times and the limits of the places where they would live. He did this so that they would look for him, and perhaps find him as they felt around for him. Yet God is actually not far from any one of us; as someone has said, 'In him we live and move and exist.' It is as some of your poets have said, 'We too are his children.' Since we are God's children, we should not suppose that his nature is anything like an image of gold or silver or stone, shaped by human art and skill. God has overlooked the times when people did not know him, but now he commands all of them everywhere to turn away from their evil ways. For he has fixed a day in which he will judge the whole world with justice by means of a man he has chosen. He has given proof of this to everyone by raising that man from death!" When they heard Paul speak about a raising from death, some of them made fun of him, but others said, "We want to hear you speak about this again." And so Paul left the meeting.

Deeper Dive

- What is Paul's level of acceptance of the religious practices in Athens?
- How does Paul's Intellection inform his innovative approach with the philosophers on Mars Hill?
- How does taking the time to think about and understand another person's beliefs and environment help us find common ground to share God's message?
- What areas of study might stimulate your thinking and make you more effective in your organization?

Challenge: Carve out time on a weekly basis to think about what God has been teaching you and share those insights with others.

Appreciation: Encourage a person with the Intellection strength to spend time writing down his or her thoughts as a way to refine and clarify the thinking process.

ENGAGE YOUR STRENGTHS STORIES

Stan Endicott—*Vice-President, Slingshot Group*

My dad flew Hellcats in World War II and to this day has a zest for living. He taught me much about life and instilled in me a commitment to excellence. He also encouraged me not to shy away from an inquiring approach to growth and learning. Words like "thinking," "reflective," and "musing" describe me well. When I have time to ponder and process, wisdom and clarity result. One of the things I most appreciate about my dad is that he gave me a love for being "curious." Over time, I have come to realize that I love to ask questions. This has paid huge dividends in my relationship with my wife Connie, my children, and especially my seven grandkids!

For many years, I was known as a Worship Pastor and Music Producer. Eight years ago, I helped start the Slingshot Group where I serve as a partner and lead our Coaching division. My heart is for mentoring, "aiming," and training young leaders. My Intellection talent helps me to do this effectively. It enables me to solve problems, develop ideas, and understand other people's feelings. I enjoy time for musing and introspection. In a sense, I can be my own best companion, as I pose myself questions and try out answers to see how they sound. But on the other hand, I like to drill deep and plumb the depths in relationship. That is why I choose to journey with others and find coaching so rewarding. The combination of reflection and asking questions seems to help free others to discover their talents and engage their strengths. It is a very exciting process.

I find a glimpse of this Intellection talent in action when the apostle Paul was interacting with the Areopagus on Mars Hill in Acts 17: *"Paul stood up in front of the city council and said, 'I see that in every way you Athenians are very religious. For as I walked through your city and looked at the places where you worship, I found an altar on which is written, 'To an Unknown God.' That which you worship, then, even though you do not know it, is what I now proclaim to you. God, who made the world and everything in it . . .'"* (vv. 22-24). Paul must have had Intellection, for he was able to help those on Mars Hill "stretch" to discover a new way to answer the questions they struggled with in the depths of their beings—questions that matter, questions about life. Their response in verse 32 said it all, "*Others said, 'We want to hear you speak about this again.'"*

Learner

Learner Strength Highlight – *People strong in the Learner theme have a great desire to learn and want to continuously improve. In particular, the process of learning, rather than the outcome, excites them.*

Scriptural Support for the Learner Strength

Daniel 1.3-6 — The king ordered Ashpenaz, his chief official, to select from among the Israelite exiles some young men of the royal family and of the noble families. They had to be handsome, intelligent, well-trained, quick to learn, and free from physical defects, so that they would be qualified to serve in the royal court. Ashpenaz was to teach them to read and write the Babylonian language. The king also gave orders that every day they were to be given the same food and wine as the members of the royal court. After three years of this training they were to appear before the king. Among those chosen were Daniel, Hananiah, Mishael, and Azariah, all of whom were from the tribe of Judah.

Matthew 11.29, 30 — "Take my yoke and put it on you, and learn from me, because I am gentle and humble in spirit; and you will find rest. For the yoke I will give you is easy, and the load I will put on you is light."

Colossians 1.9, 10 — For this reason we have always prayed for you, ever since we heard about you. We ask God to fill you with the knowledge of his will, with all the wisdom and understanding that his Spirit gives. Then you will be able to live as the Lord wants and will always do what pleases him. Your lives will produce all kinds of good deeds, and you will grow in your knowledge of God.

2 Timothy 3.14-17 — But as for you, continue in the truths that you were taught and firmly believe. You know who your teachers were, and you remember that ever since you were a child, you have known the Holy Scriptures, which are able to give you the wisdom that leads to salvation through faith in Christ Jesus. All Scripture is inspired by God and is useful for teaching the truth, rebuking error, correcting faults, and giving instruction for right living, so that the person who serves God may be fully qualified and equipped to do every kind of good deed.

Mary — a Consummate Learner

Luke 10.38-42 — As Jesus and his disciples went on their way, he came to a village where a woman named Martha welcomed him in her home. She had a sister named Mary, who sat down at the feet of the Lord and listened to his teaching. Martha was upset over all the work she had to do, so she came and said, "Lord, don't you care that my sister has left me to do all the work by myself? Tell her to come and help me!" The Lord answered her, "Martha, Martha! You are worried and troubled over so many things, but just one is needed. Mary has chosen the right thing, and it will not be taken away from her."

Deeper Dive

- On what is Martha focused? What is Mary's focus?
- Why does Jesus react to Martha as he does? What does Jesus mean by: "Mary has chosen the right thing that will not be taken away from her?"
- How can you choose the right thing that will not be taken away from you?
- Share a time when you were very excited about learning something new.

Challenge: Commit to learning something new about God from the Bible every day.

Appreciation: Ask a Learner to share something new he or she is learning about God.

ENGAGE YOUR STRENGTHS STORIES

Shellie Kelly—*Financial Management Analyst, Former Military Spouse, Wife, Mother*

Learning and gaining knowledge is as natural to me as breathing—and just as necessary. I have a compelling need to know and to understand. In fact, not knowing or not understanding is incredibly frustrating for me. Not making progress or improving can be a source of frustration as well. This holds true for both my spiritual life and the roles and responsibilities I have here on this earth.

I truly enjoy the challenge of learning a new task. This willingness to learn and gain new skills has been essential in my life. My husband served 26 years in the United States Army and, as a military spouse, I was called upon to serve in a myriad of roles and to perform many diverse tasks. Rarely were these roles or tasks ones in which I had much experience. However, each opportunity, whether it was learning to be a wife or mother, or learning tax laws and public accounting, or leading women's ministries, or teaching Bible study, or designing learning experiences for adults, or public speaking, or presenting various Army trainings, or learning governmental accounting, gave me the chance to master a new skill and to grow into the woman God intended.

I have often wondered why I am so drawn to learning. Why is it so exciting? Why not stick with something I know and have mastered?

Through *Engage Your Strengths* and StrengthsFinder®, I discovered that Learner is one of my top five talents. God made me to pursue learning. He gave me the gift of loving to learn new things! He made me to be a person not satisfied with the status quo, one that craves progress and improvement. He put in me the desire for new knowledge and experiences. He has also used my love of learning to equip and encourage ministry team members to adopt new and different ways of training.

God also gifted me to love learning of him and his ways. I pray often that I could be like Mary (Luke 10.38-42), who sat at Jesus' feet, listened to his teaching, and learned from him. Like Mary, I want to choose the one thing that is needed, the right thing that will not be taken away. What a marvelous example from Scripture to illustrate the life of a Learner.

Maximizer

Maximizer Strength Highlight – *People strong in the Maximizer theme focus on strengths as a way to stimulate personal and group excellence. They seek to transform something strong into something superb.*

Scriptural Support for the Maximizer Strength

Numbers 18.28-30 — You are to give this special contribution for the Lord to Aaron the priest. Give it from the best that you receive. When you have presented the best part, you may keep the rest, just as the farmer keeps what is left after he makes his offering.

2 Corinthians 8.7 — You are so rich in all you have: in faith, speech, and knowledge, in your eagerness to help and in your love for us. And so we want you to be generous also in this service of love.

Maximizer in the Parable of the Talents

Matthew 25.14-29 — "At that time the Kingdom of heaven will be like this. Once there was a man who was about to leave home on a trip; he called his servants and put them in charge of his property. He gave to each one according to his ability: to one he gave five thousand gold coins, to another he gave two thousand, and to another he gave one thousand. Then he left on his trip. The servant who had received five thousand coins went at once and invested his money and earned another five thousand. In the same way the servant who had received two thousand coins earned another two thousand. But the servant who had received one thousand coins went off, dug a hole in the ground, and hid his master's money. After a long time the master of those servants came back and settled accounts with them. The servant who had received five thousand coins came in and handed over the other five thousand. 'You gave me five thousand coins, sir,' he said. 'Look!

Here are another five thousand that I have earned.' 'Well done, you good and faithful servant!' said his master. 'You have been faithful in managing small amounts, so I will put you in charge of large amounts. Come on in and share my happiness!' Then the servant who had been given two thousand coins came in and said, 'You gave me two thousand coins, sir. Look! Here are another two thousand that I have earned.' 'Well done, you good and faithful servant!' said his master. 'You have been faithful in managing small amounts, so I will put you in charge of large amounts. Come on in and share my happiness!' Then the servant who had received one thousand coins came in and said, 'Sir, I know you are a hard man; you reap harvests where you did not plant, and you gather crops where you did not scatter seed. I was afraid, so I went off and hid your money in the ground. Look! Here is what belongs to you.' 'You bad and lazy servant!' his master said. 'You knew, did you, that I reap harvests where I did not plant, and gather crops where I did not scatter seed? Well, then, you should have deposited my money in the bank, and I would have received it all back with interest when I returned. Now, take the money away from him and give it to the one who has ten thousand coins. For to every person who has something, even more will be given, and he will have more than enough; but the person who has nothing, even the little that he has will be taken away from him.'"

Deeper Dive

- Why do you think the master gave a different number of coins to the three servants? What do you think he expected them to do with the coins?
- Why did he react to each of the three servants the way he did?
- Name a time when you expected great things from another person. How did you feel when your expectations were exceeded? How did you feel if your expectations were not met?

- Share a time in your life when you achieved excellence that others recognized and appreciated.

Challenge: Clearly communicate your expectations for improvement and excellence to others.

Appreciation: Ask the Maximizer how they would make things best.

ENGAGE YOUR STRENGTHS STORIES

Eric Schultz –*Executive Business Leader and Entrepreneur*

Each new day provides an opportunity for constant improvement. I can remember in my early adulthood a mindset of "forward movement" consuming me. This innate life theme has spurred my desire for growth as a servant of Christ, husband, father, entrepreneur and business leader. As long as I remember, the concepts of innovation and improvement have intrigued me. I am energized in the organizations I lead to take something good and move it into the realm of great. However, a Maximizer often sounds like a difficult boss—but, I would not have it any other way.

Good enough never is. There is a push, no a pull, that continuously draws me to motivate myself, individuals, teams and businesses toward the unquenchable goal of excellence. In a simple conversation with team members, the Maximizer theme allows me to hear strengths expressed in the nuances of the simplest conversations. "How can I leverage this person's abilities as part of a team?" Or, "How can I tap into potential that they have not fully experienced?" The ministry field to which the Lord has called me are the businesses where I am involved. In this context, I am burdened by the reality that the relationships and resources gained through the course of generating a profit are to be invested for a Kingdom-minded return.

I want nothing more than to hear, "Well done, my good and faithful servant!" I have been blessed with a wife who loves the Lord and me, relationships that are supportive and influential, and an ability to build and lead businesses. Whether I consider myself the servant with two thousand coins or the servant with five thousand coins is irrelevant. Instead, Maximizer, as demonstrated powerfully in the parable of the talents (Matthew 25.14-30), is about creating the highest return on that which I've been given. Am I leveraging every resource, every relationship and every ounce of my created "being" to generate a lasting return for my Master? Or have I buried, out of fear, anything he has loaned me for my short time here on Earth?

Positivity

Positivity Strength Highlight — *People strong in the Positivity theme have an enthusiasm that is contagious. They are upbeat and can get others excited about what they are going to do.*

Scriptural Support for the Positivity Strength

Proverbs 17.22 — Being cheerful keeps you healthy. It is slow death to be gloomy all the time.

Nehemiah 8.10 — "Now go home and have a feast. Share your food and wine with those who don't have enough. Today is holy to our Lord, so don't be sad. The joy that the Lord gives you will make you strong."

Luke 15.32 — "But we had to celebrate and be happy, because your brother was dead, but now he is alive; he was lost, but now he has been found."

1 Thessalonians 5.16-18 — Be joyful always, pray at all times, be thankful in all circumstances. This is what God wants from you in your life in union with Christ Jesus.

The Psalmist, Freely Expressing his Positivity

Psalm 100 — Sing to the Lord, all the world! Worship the Lord with joy; come before him with happy songs! Acknowledge that the Lord is God. He made us, and we belong to him; we are his people, we are his flock. Enter the Temple gates with thanksgiving; go into its courts with praise. Give thanks to him and praise him. The Lord is good; his love is eternal and his faithfulness lasts forever.

Deeper Dive

- What does the Psalmist encourage the readers to do?
- Why does the Psalmist encourage the readers to do this?
- How do you feel after you enthusiastically read this Psalm aloud?
- Share a time when you were down and someone encouraged you to have a more positive view of the situation. How can you encourage someone who seems down to be more positive?

Challenge: Use your positivity and enthusiasm to focus others on the awesomeness of God.

Appreciation: Consult someone with Positivity when you or others need encouragement or need your spirits lifted.

ENGAGE YOUR STRENGTHS STORIES

Arthur C. Pace—*U.S. Army Chaplain (Colonel), Retired*

As long as I can remember, I have always been "the glass is half full" kind of guy. My parents remark that I was one of the happiest children they had ever seen. As I grew up, I was convinced that most people have the kind of day, or sometimes even life, that they make their minds up to have. I also decided that, to the degree that I could, I would be a positive influence on those around me. This ultimately led to a call to ministry. As I pastored a church, and later served in the Army, I saw the powerful impact this attitude can have upon others. My children often joke about the endless praise and encouragement I would dole upon them, yet they seek it now when things get tough even though they are adults. My wife enjoys my ability to find humor where one would least expect it. In the Army, I was known as a team builder.

Through *Engage Your Strengths*, I learned that this strength is called Positivity. That fits me like a glove. I am naturally enthusiastic and generally optimistic. I am often viewed as a comedian, and some say I do not take things seriously. But, they are wrong. I try not to take things any more or less seriously than they need to be taken! I seek to inspire others to have a positive attitude and to enjoy, as much as possible, the task at hand. I do this through praise, recognition and humor. I cannot always lighten the load that some must carry, but I try to encourage each individual. It is important to me that my team tell others that they look forward to coming to work. I have found Positivity has allowed me to lead teams that seemed to accomplish the impossible, all with less stress and more enjoyment. The positive atmosphere unleashed the creativity and energy within each team member. I am big on promoting my team and their projects. My professional motto: praise in public, criticize in private. Above all, have fun.

When I was at a challenging point in my life, I was struck by the words of the apostle John, "*The light shines in the darkness, and the darkness has not overcome it*" (John 1.5, NIV). I linked that to the saying, "Better to light one candle than to curse the darkness." I saw Positivity as a light that I am privileged to shine into the lives of those around me. It is my strength. It is my calling. I have also found encouragement from the apostle Paul, who commanded the church to demonstrate positivity by saying, "*Be joyful always, pray at all times, be thankful in all circumstances. This is what God wants from you in your life in union with Christ Jesus*" (1 Thessalonians 5.16-18). I mean, who am I to argue with apostles?

Relator

Relator Strength Highlight – *People strong in the Relator theme enjoy close relationships with others. They find deep satisfaction in working hard with friends to achieve a goal.*

Scriptural Support for the Relator Strength

1 Samuel 18.3 — Jonathan swore eternal friendship with David because of his deep affection for him.

Proverbs 18.24 — Some friendships do not last, but some friends are more loyal than brothers.

Philippians 2.22 — And you yourselves know how he has proved his worth, how he and I, like a son and his father, have worked together for the sake of the gospel.

Elijah and Elisha Shared the Relator Strength

2 Kings 2.1-12 — The time came for the Lord to take Elijah up to heaven in a whirlwind. Elijah and Elisha set out from Gilgal, and on the way Elijah said to Elisha, "Now stay here; the Lord has ordered me to go to Bethel." But Elisha answered, "I swear by my loyalty to the living Lord and to you that I will not leave you." So they went on to Bethel. A group of prophets who lived there went to Elisha and asked him, "Do you know that the Lord is going to take your master away from you today?" "Yes, I know," Elisha answered. "But let's not talk about it." Then Elijah said to Elisha, "Now stay here; the Lord has ordered me to go to Jericho." But Elisha answered, "I swear by my loyalty to the living Lord and to you that I will not leave you." So they went on to Jericho. A group of prophets who lived there went to Elisha and asked him, "Do you know that the Lord is going to take your

master away from you today?" "Yes, I know," Elisha answered. "But let's not talk about it." Then Elijah said to Elisha, "Now stay here; the Lord has ordered me to go to the Jordan River." But Elisha answered, "I swear by my loyalty to the living Lord and to you that I will not leave you." So they went on, and fifty of the prophets followed them to the Jordan. Elijah and Elisha stopped by the river, and the fifty prophets stood a short distance away. Then Elijah took off his cloak, rolled it up, and struck the water with it; the water divided, and he and Elisha crossed to the other side on dry ground. There, Elijah said to Elisha, "Tell me what you want me to do for you before I am taken away." "Let me receive the share of your power that will make me your successor," Elisha answered. "That is a difficult request to grant," Elijah replied. "But you will receive it if you see me as I am being taken away from you; if you don't see me, you won't receive it." They kept talking as they walked on; then suddenly a chariot of fire pulled by horses of fire came between them, and Elijah was taken up to heaven by a whirlwind. Elisha saw it and cried out to Elijah, "My father, my father! Mighty defender of Israel! You are gone!" And he never saw Elijah again. In grief Elisha tore his cloak in two.

Deeper Dive

- Why do you think it is important for Elisha to remain by Elijah's side, and how do you think Elisha felt when Elijah told him to remain behind?
- Why didn't Elisha want to talk to the other prophets about Elijah's departure?
- Why do you think God sent a chariot of fire? How do you think Elisha felt after Elijah was taken up in a whirlwind?
- Name a special time you have had with your close friends that served to deepen your relationship.

Challenge: Explain to your friends how important they are to you and how much you enjoy spending time with them in work and in play.

Appreciation: Encourage a Relator to work on a project with a small group of committed friends.

ENGAGE YOUR STRENGTHS STORIES

Tracy Larson—*Church Planter, Player/Coach*

When I first got my results back from taking the *Engage Your Strengths* assessment, I was sure it was wrong. My number one result was Relator. Relator is a person who is especially talented in enjoying close relationships with others. Now if you knew me as I know me, I am shallow when it comes to relationships. I had never seen myself as a person who enjoys close relationships. When I was younger, I built many walls to protect myself from being hurt. As a result, I "became" shallow, protective, and defensive in offering myself to others.

Over a period of time, I did find "a few" with whom I could develop a genuine friendship. My wife was probably the most influential person in my life to help me see myself as a Relator. She was loyal, faithful, always there for me. She loved me for me, and always affirmed that to me. As I began to open up and be vulnerable, she handled my heart very carefully. Through her actions, I was able to open up to others and find the value in genuine and authentic relationships.

As a Relator, I am comfortable with intimacy and I deliberately encourage a deep relationship. I want to understand others' feelings, their goals, their fears, and their dreams, and I want them to understand mine. The difficulty or misunderstanding seems to come when I begin to develop a relationship. I have candor, an openness and honesty about myself. I find this makes the other person guarded. While I am opening up my life saying, "This is me, this is who I am," I am also saying to them, "now show me who you are." This makes others uncomfortable. Most people wish to disclose "little pieces" as they move forward in a relationship until they are certain it is a safe relationship. Through the years, I have learned to be aware of this quality and have taken authenticity a little more slowly.

I have also found that a person can only have a few deep relationships. As for me, those only happen with people who are going after the same pursuits in life. When I consider a life verse focusing on the Relator strength, I consider 1 Samuel 18.3, Jonathan and David forged an eternal friendship due to deep affection.

Responsibility

Responsibility Strength Highlight – *People strong in the Responsibility theme take psychological ownership of what they say they will do. They are committed to stable values such as honesty and loyalty.*

Scriptural Support for the Responsibility Strength

Proverbs 22.1 — If you have to choose between a good reputation and great wealth, choose a good reputation.

Matthew 25.34-40 — "Then the King will say to the people on his right, 'Come, you that are blessed by my Father! Come and possess the kingdom which has been prepared for you ever since the creation of the world. I was hungry and you fed me, thirsty and you gave me a drink; I was a stranger and you received me in your homes, naked and you clothed me; I was sick and you took care of me, in prison and you visited me.' The righteous will then answer him, 'When, Lord, did we ever see you hungry and feed you, or thirsty and give you a drink? When did we ever see you a stranger and welcome you in our homes, or naked and clothe you? When did we ever see you sick or in prison, and visit you?' The King will reply, 'I tell you, whenever you did this for one of the least important of these followers of mine, you did it for me!'"

James 1.22 — Do not deceive yourselves by just listening to his word; instead, put it into practice.

Daniel Takes Responsibility

Daniel 6.1-5 — Darius decided to appoint a hundred and twenty governors to hold office throughout his empire. In addition, he chose Daniel and two others to supervise the governors and to look after the king's interests.

Daniel soon showed that he could do better work than the other supervisors or the governors. Because he was so outstanding, the king considered putting him in charge of the whole empire. Then the other supervisors and the governors tried to find something wrong with the way Daniel administered the empire, but they couldn't, because Daniel was reliable and did not do anything wrong or dishonest. They said to each other, "We are not going to find anything of which to accuse Daniel unless it is something in connection with his religion."

Deeper Dive

- What causes Darius to choose Daniel to look after his interests?
- How does Daniel's responsibility affect the other supervisors and governors? Why?
- How are people who have Responsibility perceived in your group?
- What makes them so effective, and how could this negatively impact their work life balance?

Challenge: Carefully select areas of responsibility that utilize your expertise and maximize your team's effectiveness.

Appreciation: Protect the person with Responsibility from taking on too much.

ENGAGE YOUR STRENGTHS STORIES

Angel Mansberger—*Gallup® Faith Practice Strengths Coach*

My senior year in high school, I was voted "Most Likely to Succeed." Even as a teenager, others saw me as honest, loyal and following tasks to completion. What I did not realize then was that God created me with "stick-to-itiveness!" In other words, I will stick with a commitment to its completion. Now, I recognize this God-given strength as Responsibility. As a chaplain's wife, women's ministry leader, and educator, I strive to live in such a way that others respect, trust and depend on me. Giving my word means I will work long hours to get a job done. It also means I am asked to take on tasks because others know I will be dependable. I have had to learn the important skill of saying "no," so I will not become overwhelmed.

Responsibility means I take ownership of what I say I will do. For example, the statement, "I'll be praying for you," is not a cliché. It is a commitment. In my early adulthood, my pastor shared a sermon about using this phrase. He told us not to say you are going to pray for someone if you are not going to actually do it. This instruction resonated with me. I have a deep desire to keep my promises, which means I will not use this phrase unless I follow through with my prayer commitment. In fact, each commitment I make comes after determining I can successfully carry the task to completion. My strong sense of responsibility is woven into all I do.

The prophet Daniel was reliable, honest, and hardworking. In Daniel 6.4, no one could find fault in how he handled the affairs of the Kingdom. Daniel lived his life to glorify the Lord. My prayer is that I can glorify the Lord in my family, ministry and workplace. Like Daniel, I want to live above reproach and be a person of integrity. To accomplish this, I must start each day asking God to help me do what I say I will do. In my own strength, I will let others down. I need God's strength and power. I need the Holy Spirit to fill and guide me.

Restorative

Restorative Strength Highlight – *People strong in the Restorative theme are adept at dealing with problems. They are good at figuring out what is wrong and resolving it.*

Scriptural Support for the Restorative Strength

Psalms 23 — The Lord is my shepherd; I have everything I need. He lets me rest in fields of green grass and leads me to quiet pools of fresh water. He gives me new strength. He guides me in the right paths, as he has promised. Even if I go through the deepest darkness, I will not be afraid, Lord, for you are with me. Your shepherd's rod and staff protect me. You prepare a banquet for me, where all my enemies can see me; you welcome me as an honored guest and fill my cup to the brim. I know that your goodness and love will be with me all my life; and your house will be my home as long as I live.

Galatians 6.1 — My friends, if someone is caught in any kind of wrongdoing, those of you who are spiritual should set him right; but you must do it in a gentle way. And keep an eye on yourselves, so that you will not be tempted, too.

Restoration at Levi's Banquet

Luke 5.27-32 — After this, Jesus went out and saw a tax collector named Levi, sitting in his office. Jesus said to him, "Follow me." Levi got up, left everything, and followed him. Then Levi had a big feast in his house for Jesus, and among the guests was a large number of tax collectors and other people. Some Pharisees and some teachers of the Law who belonged to their group complained to Jesus' disciples. "Why do you eat and drink with tax collectors and other outcasts?" they asked. Jesus answered them, "People who are well do not need a doctor, but only those who are sick. I have not come to call respectable people to repent, but outcasts."

Deeper Dive

- What does Jesus see in the tax collector that the Pharisees do not?
- Why does Jesus go out of his way to eat with those on the outskirts of Jewish society? What does that tell us about how we should endeavor to treat those who are outside of your group?
- What is the significance of Jesus' statement, "Follow Me?" How do we obey Jesus?
- How can you restore those around you to right standing with the Lord?

Challenge: Proactively identify and solve problems and seek God's direction to expand your sphere of influence.

Appreciation: Go out of your way to recognize a problem solver and encourage them to take another step to continually disciple those involved.

ENGAGE YOUR STRENGTHS STORIES

Rev. Dr. Bagudekia Alobeyo—*Director, "She's My Sister" Program, Restoration Ministries*

I am naturally able to identify myself with the sufferings of others and have always been driven to lift up people who are experiencing various burdens. I enjoy being involved in problem-solving, especially when people do not see any way out. My Restorative strength manifests itself when I see people facing challenges. I always feel obligated to discuss them and find a way toward a resolution. I love to review a conversation, meeting, or an event in my mind and figure out how to overcome any tension or rough spots between people. These areas of disconnect don't drain me at all. In fact, they energize me. This theme allows me to see areas of disagreement and gives me the courage to speak to others in order to provide resolution.

In my role as a husband, father and grandfather, my family members easily approach me for advice and direction. My grandchildren tell me that they are sad when I have to be away on a trip for more than a week. In high school, my classmates called me "Monk" because I was so often involved in promoting reconciliation between people in conflict. As a pastor, the Restorative strength made my ministry enjoyable and helpful. I especially enjoyed receiving young, single and married people for pastoral counseling. Some church members used to call me a man of "salama," the Kiswahili word for "peace." As a Bible school principal, both students and teachers frequently used to set appointments with me to talk about their personal issues. When I served as vice-president of my denomination in Democratic Republic of Congo, I played a crucial role in bringing people together when the church was experiencing hatred and was in danger of schism.

There are so many Scriptures that impact me and affirm my Restorative strength. I am especially drawn to 2 Corinthians 13.11 (NIV), "*Finally, brothers and sisters, rejoice! Strive for full restoration, encourage one another, be of one mind, live in peace. And the God of love and peace will be with you.*" Another powerful Scripture is Isaiah 49.8 (NIV), "*This is what the Lord says: 'In the time of my favor I will answer you, and in the day of salvation I will help you; I will keep you and will make you to be a covenant for the people, to restore the land and to reassign its desolate inheritances.'*"

Self-Assurance

> **Self-Assurance Strength Highlight** — *People strong in the Self-Assurance theme feel confident in their ability to manage their own lives. They possess an inner compass that gives them confidence that their decisions are right.*

Scriptural Support for the Self-Assurance Strength

Matthew 3.1-6 — At that time John the Baptist came to the desert of Judea and started preaching. "Turn away from your sins," he said, "because the Kingdom of heaven is near!" John was the man the prophet Isaiah was talking about when he said, "Someone is shouting in the desert, 'Prepare a road for the Lord; make a straight path for him to travel!'" John's clothes were made of camel's hair; he wore a leather belt around his waist, and his food was locusts and wild honey. People came to him from Jerusalem, from the whole province of Judea, and from all over the country near the Jordan River. They confessed their sins, and he baptized them in the Jordan.

2 Timothy 1.12b — But I am still full of confidence, because I know whom I have trusted, and I am sure that he is able to keep safe until that Day what he has entrusted to me.

Esther Uses Self-Assurance to Save a Nation

Esther 4.5-17 — Then she called Hathach, one of the palace eunuchs appointed as her servant by the king, and told him to go to Mordecai and find out what was happening and why. Hathach went to Mordecai in the city square at the entrance of the palace. Mordecai told him everything that had happened to him and just how much money Haman had promised to put into the royal treasury if all the Jews were killed. He gave Hathach a copy of the proclamation that had been issued in Susa, ordering the destruction of the Jews. Mordecai asked him to take it to Esther, explain the situation to her, and have her go and plead with the king and beg him to have mercy on her people. Hathach did this, and Esther gave him this message to take back to Mordecai: "If anyone, man or woman, goes to the inner courtyard and sees the king without being summoned, that person must die. That is the law; everyone, from the king's advisers to the people in the provinces, knows that. There is only one way to get around this law: if the king holds out his gold scepter to someone, then that person's life is spared. But it has been a month since the king sent for me." When Mordecai received Esther's message, he sent her this warning: "Don't imagine that you are safer than any other Jew just because you are in the royal palace. If you keep quiet at a time like this, help will come from heaven to the Jews, and they will be saved, but you will die and your father's family will come to an end. Yet who knows —maybe it was for a time like this that you were made queen!" Esther sent Mordecai this reply: "Go and get all the Jews in Susa together; hold a fast and pray for me. Don't eat or drink anything for three days and nights. My servant women and I will be doing the same. After that, I will go to the king, even though it is against the law. If I must die for doing it, I will die." Mordecai then left and did everything that Esther had told him to do.

Deeper Dive

- What are the barriers that Esther faces in pleading with the king?
- How much is Esther willing to risk to save the Jewish people?
- How much are you willing to risk for God?
- Tell about a time when you were sure that your decision was correct.

Challenge: Explain how your inner compass guides you to do the right thing.

Appreciation: Encourage a person with Self-Assurance to explain how they came to their steadfast decisions.

ENGAGE YOUR STRENGTHS STORIES

Rev. John Hansen—*Lead Pastor CENTERPOINT Church, Murrieta, CA*

I am a leader, and one of my top five signature themes is Self-Assurance. I have found myself in leadership roles throughout my life – not because I was seeking out leadership; but simply because, in many circumstances, I have seen the best path forward and have naturally exerted influence in that direction. I have done this almost automatically. In any situation in which there is uncertainty, I have a strong sense of what needs to happen – and a strong conviction that my perspective and course of action is truly the best and most helpful way to go.

I have a strong anchor in my faith, and that is foundational for my sense of self-assurance. I often sense that God has given me insight and direction for my own life and for the circumstances in which I am leading. When I have a sense that God has spoken to me, I feel resolute and am not easily deterred! In fact, I have often found myself in circumstances where I've felt so assured about the direction I needed to take that I have been willing to step out in faith toward that direction, even if it would result in potential personal loss or loss of support from others.

As one who has Self-Assurance, I experience that strength as something rooted in my faith. There are times when I feel resolve as deeply as Esther did. She said to Mordecai, "*I'll go to the king, even though it's forbidden. If I die, I die.*" (Esther 4.16, The Message). I pastor a church and, at one point, I felt the church needed a new name. I believe I heard from God about the matter! Many people stood against me and threatened to leave. They tried to dissuade me, proclaiming that the church would fall apart if I continued on this path. My Self-Assurance strength was deeply engaged in this matter; the name would be changed, and it was absolutely the right thing to do, even if those people left, and even if the decision led to my demise. Almost three years later, the church has more than doubled in size and is thriving under the new name! I had such a confident, deep 'knowing' that this would in fact be the result! I felt the way 2 Timothy 1.12 calls me to feel: "*But I am still full of confidence, because I know whom I have trusted, and I am sure that he is able to keep safe until that Day what he has entrusted to me.*"

Significance

Significance Strength Highlight — *People strong in the Significance theme want to be very important in the eyes of others. They are independent and want to be recognized. They are motivated by a driving force to produce transformational, lasting change — leaving a legacy.*

Scriptural Support for the Significance Strength

1 Samuel 9.1, 2 — There was a wealthy and influential man named Kish, from the tribe of Benjamin; he was the son of Abiel and grandson of Zeror, and belonged to the family of Becorath, a part of the clan of Aphiah. He had a son named Saul, a handsome man in the prime of life. Saul was a foot taller than anyone else in Israel and more handsome as well.

John 10.10 — "The thief comes only in order to steal, kill, and destroy. I have come in order that you might have life — life in all its fullness."

1 Corinthians 4.15,16 — For even if you have ten thousand guardians in your Christian life, you have only one father. For in your life in union with Christ Jesus I have become your father by bringing the Good News to you. I beg you, then, to follow my example.

A Different Twist on Significance

Matthew 5.13-16 — "You are like salt for the whole human race. But if salt loses its saltiness, there is no way to make it salty again. It has become worthless, so it is thrown out and people trample on it. You are like light for the whole world. A city built on a hill cannot be hid. No one lights a lamp and puts it under a bowl; instead it is put on the lamp stand, where it gives light for everyone in the house. In the same way your light must shine before people, so that they will see the good things you do and praise your Father in heaven."

Deeper Dive

- Why do you think Jesus uses the images of salt and light to make his point in this passage? What other things could he use to make his point?
- What biblical characters are known for their significance? How do you think King Saul (in 1 Samuel 9) is significant?
- Have you ever been motivated and influenced by the perceptions of others? If so, describe how.
- How true is the following statement to you –"My work is my way of life?"

Challenge: Decide what your legacy will be and take incremental steps to make it happen.

Appreciation: Encourage those with the Significance talent to continue to be known and appreciated for the unique strengths they bring to life.

ENGAGE YOUR STRENGTHS STORIES

Rev. Jeb Shore—*Television Sports Reporter, Radio News Anchor, Pastor*

As a reporter, it appears that I've never met a microphone I didn't like. As a television sports reporter in Columbia, South Carolina, I interviewed the greatest athletes and coaches in the world on a consistent basis. I really enjoyed thinking of the best ways to communicate a story to thousands. I was passionate about what I did. I would consistently ask God for guidance and he was faithful. I earned two regional Associated Press Awards for my reporting. That role was a huge part of my life for nearly six years. I had very little time for anything else. As a result, I wanted more and more success. I craved affirmation from my boss and viewers. It seemed deep within me I wanted to be recognized, heard, and valued.

I have learned that Significance is one of my dominant talent themes. In turn, I seek to have an impact on people, groups, and society as a whole. I am motivated by an intense desire to be recognized, and as a result, I keep reaching for the stars. It is through my Significance theme that I'm pulled upward, away from the mediocre and toward the exceptional. I have come to realize that I want the world to be a better place because I was here.

The apostle Paul writes in Ephesians 2.10, "*God has made us what we are, and in our union with Christ Jesus he has created us for a life of good deeds, which he has already prepared for us to do.*" God created me for a life of good deeds. I'm so thankful that he's given me the ability to interact with anyone and speak to thousands. I also believe God calls me to leverage my God-given talents, including Significance. Matthew 5.13-16 puts a different twist on Significance, "*You are like salt for the whole human race. But if salt loses its saltiness, there is no way to make it salty again. It has become worthless, so it is thrown out and people trample on it. You are like light for the whole world. A city built on a hill cannot be hid. No one lights a lamp and puts it under a bowl; instead it is put on the lamp stand, where it gives light for everyone in the house. In the same way your light must shine before people, so that they will see the good things you do and praise your Father in heaven.*"

Making God my ultimate audience makes it possible for me to keep a proper perspective on my talents and satisfies my cravings for significance. As I recognize and celebrate the tangible expressions of God's work through others and through me, it moves me closer to the legacy I want to leave.

Strategic

Strategic Strength Highlight – *People strong in the Strategic theme create alternative ways to proceed. Faced with any given scenario, they can quickly spot the relevant patterns and issues.*

Scriptural Support for the Strategic Strength

Psalm 25.4, 5—Teach me your ways, O Lord; make them known to me. Teach me to live according to your truth, for you are my God, who saves me. I always trust in you.

1 Corinthians 10.13 — Every test that you have experienced is the kind that normally comes to people. But God keeps his promise, and he will not allow you to be tested beyond your power to remain firm; at the time you are put to the test, he will give you the strength to endure it, and so provide you with a way out.

Four Strategic Friends

Mark 2.1-12 — A few days later Jesus went back to Capernaum, and the news spread that he was at home. So many people came together that there was no room left, not even out in front of the door. Jesus was preaching the message to them when four men arrived, carrying a paralyzed man to Jesus. Because of the crowd, however, they could not get the man to him. So they made a hole in the roof right above the place where Jesus was. When they had made an opening, they let the man down, lying on his mat. Seeing how much faith they had, Jesus said to the paralyzed man, "My son, your sins are forgiven." Some teachers of the Law who were sitting there thought to themselves, "How does he dare talk like this? This is blasphemy! God is the only one who can forgive sins!" At once Jesus knew what they were thinking, so he said to them, "Why do you think such things? Is it easier to say to this paralyzed man, 'Your sins are forgiven,' or to say, 'Get up, pick up your mat, and walk?' I will prove to you, then, that the Son of Man has authority on earth to forgive sins." So he said to the paralyzed man, "I tell you, get up, pick up your mat, and go home!" While they all watched, the man got up, picked up his mat, and hurried away. They were all completely amazed and praised God, saying, "We have never seen anything like this!"

Deeper Dive

- What do you think really motivated the four friends to get the paralytic to Jesus?
- Has your Strategic talent ever prompted you to interrupt someone's talk, inconvenience an entire crowd, and 'make a hole in someone else's roof?' If so, describe what happened.
- Do you face any 'closed front doors' in your life? What are they, and how might faith in God help you confront them?
- How often do you 'see' a way when others assume there is no way?

Challenge: Use your creative anticipation, imagination, and persistence to help others consider all Kingdom possibilities.

Appreciation: Encourage those with Strategic talents to evaluate the possibilities, see patterns, and consider the whole picture to find the best route.

ENGAGE YOUR STRENGTHS STORIES

Tom Fox—*Executive Pastor and Coach, Meadowbrook Church, Ocala, FL*

So often life is full of clutter and obstacles that make finding the best route difficult. This is true in every area I have encountered over the last 21 years – family, faith and ministry. Each and every day, I find that my roles and responsibilities provide me the opportunity to help those I lead consider possibilities and evaluate alternative routes to the best solutions. As a follower of Christ, husband, father, pastor and coach I am able to use my God-given talents to invite those within my sphere of influence and care to live every day in the reality of being fearfully and wonderfully made. I live to help people move from where they are to where God wants them to be. This truly makes my heart beat fast!

The Strategic strength allows me to see patterns where others simply see complexity. As I am mindful of these patterns, I envision alternative scenarios, always asking, "What if this happened?" This recurring question helps me see, plan and prepare for future situations. I bring creative anticipation, imagination and persistence to the groups and projects I work on. Whether it is helping someone from my team or from another organization, I usually see a way when others assume there is no way. I have often been told that I can eliminate distractions, enabling others to gain a clear understanding of what is happening and why. In fact, my teams learn to quickly identify problems and generate alternatives for solving them, while determining the path that will work most efficiently.

I have often relied on Psalm 25.4, 5 to guide me, "*Teach me your ways, O Lord; make them known to me. Teach me to live according to your truth, for you are my God, who saves me. I always trust in you.*" I have also been intrigued with the four strategic friends in Mark 2.1-12. I love the part that states, "*Because of the crowd, however, they could not get the man to him. So they made a hole in the roof right above the place where Jesus was.*" (Mark 2.4) How often this comes to my mind when I have to find another way to move forward. They are great examples of being willing to consider all the possibilities. It points me to the end of 1 Corinthians 10.13, "*At the time you are put to the test, he will give you the strength to endure it, and so provide you with a way out.*"

Woo

WOO Strength Highlight – *People strong in the WOO theme love the challenge of meetings new people and winning them over. They derive satisfaction from breaking the ice and making a connection with another person.*

Scriptural Support for the WOO Strength

Matthew 9.36-38 — As he saw the crowds, his heart was filled with pity for them, because they were worried and helpless, like sheep without a shepherd. So he said to his disciples, "The harvest is large, but there are few workers to gather it in. Pray to the owner of the harvest that he will send out workers to gather in his harvest."

Colossians 4.5, 6 — Be wise in the way you act toward those who are not believers, making good use of every opportunity you have. Your speech should always be pleasant and interesting, and you should know how to give the right answer to everyone.

Hebrews 13.2 — Remember to welcome strangers in your homes. There were some who did that and welcomed angels without knowing it.

Woo for the Kingdom of God

Mark 10.13-16 — Some people brought children to Jesus for him to place his hands on them, but the disciples scolded the people. When Jesus noticed this, he was angry and said to his disciples, "Let the children come to me, and do not stop them, because the Kingdom of God belongs to such as these. I assure you that whoever does not receive the Kingdom of God like a child will never enter it." Then he took the children in his arms, placed his hands on each of them, and blessed them.

Deeper Dive

- Why did people bring their children to Jesus?
- What was the disciples' reaction? Why? How did Jesus respond to this?
- How did Jesus use this occasion to teach about the Kingdom of God? What was the teaching?
- Name a time when you experienced being warmly welcomed into a new situation. What happened to make you feel welcomed?
- How can you encourage people to receive the Kingdom of God like a child?

Challenge: Use your approachability and desire for social interaction to draw people towards Jesus and the Kingdom of God.

Appreciation: Identify outgoing, approachable people in your group, thank them, and encourage them to reach out to new people.

ENGAGE YOUR STRENGTHS STORIES

Jim Ammerman–*Spiritual Formation Pastor, Deep Creek Community Church, Punta Gorda, FL*

For as long as I can remember, meeting new people has been an adventure. Some enjoy people watching, but as a strong WOO, I quickly move from watching, to engaging and befriending new people. My desire is to find a mutual interest and to encourage people to discover their God-given purpose in life. As a result of my WOO, our family has friends and acquaintances from all walks of life. My kids enjoy these benefits when people we barely know treat us as close friends.

As a pastor, my WOO strength enables me to welcome outsiders to the church, building rapport, then connecting them to people who can help them grow. I am skilled at recruiting volunteers because I intuitively ask newcomers the right questions, gain their trust, and encourage them to join a ministry team. Finding common interests and seeking to win others over also removes barriers to evangelism. Last week I met a woman who exclaimed that she knew me and that I had "saved her." I asked her to remind me of our meeting, and she described how I talked to her after a service, prayed with her, and encouraged her to get involved at the church. Since then, she has been free of addiction issues for two years and has been following Christ. Although I met her only once, and didn't even remember her, my WOO had caused her to feel safe and to share her deepest personal challenges, so that I was able to direct her toward Christ and his people.

My WOO has also been very useful in conflict resolution. Because conflict is a normal part of relationships, I have become skilled at mediating and training others to mediate conflict. The "winning" aspect in conflict resolution removes barriers to reconciliation and identifies core values and root causes of conflict. As a WOO, I'm skilled at tactfully identifying the "elephant" in the room and carefully addressing it. In an ugly rent dispute between church members, the owner assumed the Christian tenants would be fiscally responsible, while the tenants believed the owner to be generous and understanding of their financial woes. In mediating this conflict, my "WOO-ness" helped both parties to see that I was "for" them and had their best interest at heart. I was able to gain the trust of all, help them reach a mutually agreeable resolution, and the debt was paid in less than a year. Recently, a couple I had never met came to me after a meeting, expressing hurt and frustration toward the church and their desire to leave. As a WOO, I lovingly engaged them in dialogue, disarmed their animosity and set them on a path to constructively deal with their concerns.

The life of a WOO is perfectly described in 1 Corinthians 9.19-23 (NIV), as Paul expresses his heart to "*win as many as possible.....[and to become] all things to all people so that by all means possible, I might save some....all this for the sake of the gospel.*" As a WOO, I am always seeking to engage people, whether in restaurants, airports, church foyers, or soccer fields. And, like Paul, my desire is to listen to them, find common ground, earn their trust, and, by all means possible, win as many as possible for the sake of the gospel. WOO, or "winning others over" can easily translate into winning others for Christ.

SECTION 3

Engage Your Strengths for Life

- **CHAPTER 6:** *Engage Your Strengths* Coaching Stories
- **CHAPTER 7:** Coaching Exercises
- **CHAPTER 8:** Theme Insight Cards with Balconies and Basements

For the body itself is not made up of only one part, but of many parts. If the foot were to say, "Because I am not a hand, I don't belong to the body," that would not keep it from being a part of the body. And if the ear were to say, "Because I am not an eye, I don't belong to the body," that would not keep it from being a part of the body. If the whole body were just an eye, how could it hear? And if it were only an ear, how could it smell? As it is, however, God put every different part in the body just as he wanted it to be. There would not be a body if it were all only one part! As it is, there are many parts but one body.

1 Corinthians 12.14-20

Chapter 6

EYS FOR LIFE COACHING STORIES

Over the past five years there have been hundreds of *Engage Your Strengths* coaches trained. We asked a number of them to provide examples of transformation – in individual lives and in churches and units as a whole. We have chosen the following eight stories and trust they will inspire and challenge you.

Permission to Be Task-Oriented

Mary had been a church planter's wife for over 20 years. She was the type of person who was always keeping a list and checking it off because of the many demands in her life, which included a job and two children as well as the church. Mary seemed to always find the most efficient way to get a job done quickly with the least resources. This had been a great help because most of the time they were doing ministry on a shoestring budget and with less personnel than they needed. Mary and her husband worked as a team and they effectively "thought through" ministry and personal decisions together. Yet, in spite of their ministries being successful, Mary always had the feeling that she wasn't enough of the "touchy-feely" pastor's wife that she thought she should be. Mary was kind and caring, but she always felt driven to "do" ministry rather than sit and listen to people's problems or just "be" with them. Her mind was always racing toward the next thing on her list that needed to be done. She'd rather make a meal and clean it up than be the guest.

Mary came to her first coaching session with a number of thoughts and questions written down. She told me that she felt a huge relief when she read her print out. Mary's signature strengths were: Achiever, Strategic, Responsibility, Focus, and Discipline. She stated that if God had made her this way, it must be ok for her to be a busy, task-oriented pastor's wife. She went on to inform me that her husband had three talents in Relationship Building, one in Influencing and one in Strategic. Together, they made a dynamite team. He had the patience with his Relator and Adaptability themes to take care of people's needs so she could be her busy self. His Learner meant that he truly enjoyed getting to know all about the new people who came to their church. Mary was amazed that God had brought her a man with the perfect strengths to complement hers. She had felt called to ministry as a teenager and realized that her husband's strengths allowed her to do the ministry to which she felt called. Likewise, her strengths allowed her husband to be with people because she joyfully took care of most of the practical tasks that needed to be done at home and church.

Rebecca L. Puchy, *GALLUP® Certified Strengths Coach*
WOO | Maximizer | Individualization | Learner | Achiever

No Such Thing as Random or Bazaar

What a story. Bob was raised and survived his teen years in an extremely conservative religious family in rural farming America in the 1970's. Bob was most influenced by the work ethic of his family and the close community in which he lived. As was true for many 1970's teens, he rebelled against it all.

Over 40 years later, as a PhD marriage and family counselor, successful corporate franchise executive, pastor, and owner of multiple businesses, Bob asked me to coach him on his strengths. I simply said…hesitantly and reluctantly, "OK, but only if you promise to coach me afterwards." We both laughed. We've been friends for decades.

Bob's top five talents are Learner, Connectedness, Strategic, Achiever, and Communication. There isn't anything that Bob does that isn't informed. Once Bob gains new and corroborated information, he's compelled to apply and advocate its truth. When Bob learned the truth about the growing Muslim extremist nations and about some of their destructive practices, he leapt into action. He now takes multiple trips annually to Muslim dominated countries to do his part. When he learned that families were crumbling across America, he embarked on a PhD counseling program. The list goes on.

In our first coaching session, I asked Bob how he felt about his top five talent themes. Stoically, as usual, he said, "That's me." I asked, "Is any of the five especially intriguing to you?" He said, "Connectedness. It is somewhat of a foundation to the others. I have this particular religious inclination that says, 'It all makes sense and has a reason. There is no such thing as random or bazaar.'"

After some deeper conversation, I asked Bob, "Given your vast knowledge of various personality tools and placement mechanisms, how do you think your strengths should be aimed?" He said, "Most of what I do is in direct contact with people, yet I am mostly a strategic and executing guy [he read the book], I think that I'll focus [Strategic] on learning how I can help people in my counseling center. I'll use my Communication strength to find the right words to get them to achieve success and hopefully connect them to the big picture."

I said, "Okay Bob – now your turn to coach me."

Thomas J. Trageser, *GALLUP® Certified Strengths Coach*
Communication | WOO | Includer | Connectedness | Input

Appreciation for the Commitment to Excellence

Rochelle is a gifted worship leader, Bible teacher, and a strong, courageous leader in women's ministry. Over the years, I watched as she befriended one young woman after another and helped them develop their talents. She seemed to instinctively know an individual's unique talents and how to develop those talents. But, I also observed that occasionally her approach was like sand paper to some individuals because she didn't settle for mediocrity. I was eager to see the report from her Clifton StrengthsFinder® assessment. I also looked forward to unpacking her talents and coaching her through *Engage Your Strengths*.

When discussing her signature themes: Learner, Intellection, Developer, Maximizer, and Individualization, I asked her if she felt that the these accurately describe her. She hesitantly said yes. Learner, Intellection, Developer, and Individualization were easy to discern and address. However, when we began to address the Maximizer theme, Rochelle shared that she had always known just the "fixes" that were necessary to make an event or a worship experience better. Whether it was the lighting, or the sound system or the worship slides, etc., she just knew what to do. As she communicated those "fixes," more often than not, she would offend those she was trying to help. Her attempts toward excellence were only seen as picky criticism. Eventually, she became frustrated and began to despise this talent. She even asked God to take away this ability, but he didn't.

Upon seeing her signature themes on paper, she realized God intended for her to spur the body of Christ to excellence. It was important for her to fulfill her role in the body. The discovery of her signature themes helped her to embrace her Maximizer and even changed the way she prayed. She no longer asked God to take away this talent, but instead she asked him to bring out the Fruit of the Spirit—love, joy, peace, patience, kindness, goodness, faithfulness, gentleness and self-control.

Shellie Kelly, *Gallup® Faith Practice Strengths Performance Coach*
Connectedness | Individualization | Relator | Achiever | Learner

Transition to an Interdependent Team

As a doctoral student, I am occasionally asked to advise college administrators with regards to team development and leadership issues. Recently, I was asked to advise an administrator. Several of his staff had complained that their division seemed to be drifting and that they were not accomplishing much or meeting their goals.

The entire staff took the StrengthsFinder® assessment. During our next meeting, I led a short seminar on *Engage Your Strengths* and how it could be used to build strong effective teams. I also discussed their goals and what their clients expected of them with regards to the services that they offered. I showed them an Excel™ printout of their team's talent themes. Upon viewing them and discussing how their strengths were clustered, they came to the realization that, while they had a lot of strategic thinkers on their team, only a few of them were executors and, therefore, little was being accomplished. They also took note that the administrator, while a nice guy, was a researcher whose top signature theme was Ideation and it was a struggle for him to lead his team. He had been comfortable in his role as the assistant leader for some time and now found it a challenge to be the team leader. His promotion, given because he had been around for a long time, had not gone well. His current assistant, however, had Command as his top signature theme. He also had Achiever as a dominant theme and was obviously frustrated.

Soon after this consultation, the administrator retired. His former assistant became the Director. His team was soon achieving its goals and was no longer drifting. Several team members were promoted or resigned, and the new director replaced them with others who complimented his strengths. The team now relies on each other to get work done. Team members are positioned to do what he or she does best. The team has moved to be a strengths-based team with each team member understanding his/her role. The division now meets the needs of its clients.

Professor Brian Shore, *Gallup® Faith Practice Strengths Performance Coach*
Strategic | Activator | Futuristic | Ideation | Maximizer

Talent and Non-Inspirational Leadership

PVT Anderson was an Initial Entry Military Intelligence Soldier, with some college experience, who joined the military to be part of something bigger than he could be on his own. Because of his high entrance exam score, he was selected for rigorous training often found to be mentally challenging by the most scholarly students.

Due to mounting frustrations regarding his training environment, he approached me, his chaplain, following a military resiliency class. After he completed his StrengthsFinder® assessment, I scheduled a coaching session to include PVT Anderson's platoon sergeant-instructor and his battle buddy. My hope was that the new awareness of PVT Anderson's strengths would aid him in building his support system as well as assist him in deciding whether or not he could continue to serve in the military community in his current role. His signature themes were: Adaptability, Analytical, Includer, Harmony and Deliberative.

Although his top Strength was "Adaptability," I believed his other four signature themes were in conflict with his perception of the low-level motivational techniques (non-inspirational leadership) often employed in military training situations. What works for many others, i.e. threats, ridicule and verbally berating someone, would not likely work with this Soldier who had quickly drawn conclusions regarding existing trends in his training environment.

We discussed ways in which he could build his support system outside of class to compensate for the diminished experience he was having in class. In addition, I affirmed my ongoing support for the duration of his training. We discovered that he viewed his First Sergeant as an inspirational leader and arranged for him to have a discussion and more of an interpersonal role with him. He continued to work within the existing framework of the military, which aided in him obtaining an agreed upon discharge from the military without compromise to his values, military law, and desire to make a difference where he might be better suited.

Lisa Northway, *Gallup® Faith Practice Strengths Performance Coach*
Strategic | Positivity | Includer | Activator | Maximizer

Talents as the Key to Overcoming

Megan is a young lady who was in her last year of college when I coached her through *Engage Your Strengths*. She was engaged to be married and was trying to figure out what her role would be as a future pastor's wife. She was not sure she had made the right decision in her schooling degree, in light of the latest developments in her life. When she received her results, and we walked her through them, it was one of the most satisfying experiences to witness. Her Clifton StrengthsFinder® report revealed that her top talent themes included Developer, Restorative, Empathy, Adaptability, and Positivity. I asked her, "Do you enjoy working with people in a counseling setting?" I followed with, "Do you enjoy helping people find ways to improve on their lives and overcome problems?" She looked at me perplexed and went on to tell me that her major was counseling. She had always been drawn to helping others find victories in their lives as she had done in overcoming many obstacles in her's. She told me that her father was a wounded veteran and that, of all his children, she was always the one he would lean on for help.

After graduating, her husband accepted a call to be a Youth Pastor in a church. It was most satisfying to her to see how she fit in that role and how she too would have a ministry alongside them. The only difficulty was that they were moving to another part of the country far away from family. As we talked about it and she said, "It will be ok, we'll manage." I pointed out to her that her signature themes Adaptability and Positivity were really empowering her through this change.

Alfredo Gutierrez, *Gallup® Faith Practice Strengths Performance Coach*
Communication | Positivity | Activator | WOO | Belief

Leveraging Your Relator

Brian is a fearless dynamo with signature themes of Achiever, Learner, Command, Relator, and Competition. Strengths in these areas have helped him be successful, but have also caused him difficulty in relationships. He is an administrative pastor who first approached me because he was interested in bringing StrengthsFinder® to his fellow staff members. We set up a coaching plan for staff members, and Brian also signed on for coaching sessions. Always equipped with a list of tasks, Brian was determined to win by accomplishing his goals. His Competition strength functioned like pouring jet fuel onto a flaming fire. Once Brian had an interest in something new, he worked on it tirelessly from the time he started researching until the time he implemented his plan. Everyone benefitted greatly from Brian's ability to find new ways to accomplish all sorts of things, but once he decided to move forward, it could be difficult to keep up with him.

It didn't take long to realize that his Achiever, fueled by his strengths in Command and Competition, made relationships tricky. Brian's ability to relate to others is a challenge because, while Brian cares about people, he doesn't always realize how he affects them. His Relator strength is a great bridge, and during our coaching sessions, Brian learned ways to use this strength to connect with others. He learned how to connect with people and stay grounded in the present conversation when speaking with them, further enabling him to interact rather than give commands. Brian is such a fast learner that he was able to teach himself to stay in the present, focus on the language he uses (not commands), and connect to the conversation using his Relator strength. It didn't take long for Brian's relationships to become much more engaging and fulfilling. Brian is still careful to monitor his language and he knows that he will have better relationships if he says, "Could you please clean the floor when you finish painting" rather than saying, "Go clean the floor."

Kristy McAdams, *Gallup® Faith Practice Strengths Performance Coach*
Command | Activator | Input | Relator | Futuristic

Valuing Each Person's Uniqueness

Rachel was a vibrant, warm, creative individual. She was always encouraging and affirming. It seemed she never knew a stranger, always investing in others by allowing them to share their stories with her. Most thought of her as an outgoing individual, that is until she began working as a receptionist. After being there for about a year, Rachel began to change. She became withdrawn, less talkative. She began taking her lunch breaks alone in quiet places. Her inquisitiveness about others all but disappeared. I had observed Rachel through this transition and tried to get her to open up about what was going on in her life. She was always vague about what was bothering her until one day I was in her work area and saw her situation a little clearer. I began a conversation with her that ended up with her taking the Clifton StrengthsFinder® Assessment.

Rachel's results revealed that her number one strength was Individualization. As we talked about this it seemed that a light went on in her eyes. The problem she continued to encounter in her little workspace was that she overheard all the negative comments about others, usually their shortcomings. As someone talented in Individualization, Rachel saw the unique qualities of the people around her. Every time she tried to defend those individuals that she knew and was investing in, she was silenced and her opinion was not heard. She felt ignored and that her input did not matter. As time went on she began second-guessing her passion for people and her ability to see the good qualities in other people's lives. She quit sticking up for others and became despondent, frustrated, and hurt by those around her.

As someone with Individualization, Rachel was talented in seeing people's giftedness and uniqueness. Through our conversations I encouraged her that part of her role there was to help others see what she saw. As she began to do this with a little more confidence about her talent things began to change. Today Rachel is no longer overlooked and silenced; rather, she has been promoted to a supervisory role and helps to place people in the company.

Tracy Larson, *Gallup® Faith Practice Strengths Performance Coach*
Relator | Achiever | Communication | Activator | Woo

Chapter 7

COACHING EXERCISES

In this chapter you will find coaching exercises that can be used in individual, group, and presentation settings.

Here are two exercises that can be used with group coaching or in presentation settings.

Focus on You

Name	What You Get Paid to Do	Positive Hot Buttons	Two Successes	Expectations

Stand up if you:

- Talk to people in elevators, in grocery stores, on airplanes . . .
- Make the bed, pick things up, before you leave the house . . .
- Have a color-coded or otherwise organized closet . . .
- Make a list of things to do, write it down, and stick to it…
- Make list of things to do on weekends . . .
- Make a beeline to a familiar face at a big party . . .
- Need to pick someone to race while driving on the freeway
- Are accused of being "too nice" . . .
- Are accused of not being "too nice" . . .
- Asking too many questions . . .
- Are always figuring out the plot of the movie before anyone else does . . .
- Are skeptical unless given some proof . . .
- Just want everyone to get along . . .
- Are pushing the elevator button to "remind the elevator" you are there . . .

Utilize the following during individual and group coaching.

"Good At, Not So Good At" QUIZ

WRITE:

- Three things you are very good at
- Three things you are not very good at
- Which list was easier to make?
- Take a couple of minutes to share with a person next to you - your 'very good at' and 'not very good at' lists.
- Was there something on someone's "very good at" list that was on your "not very good at" list?

CSF Report First Look

> Take a look at descriptions of your Top 5
>
> Highlight the portions that best describe your dominant talents

> Highlight your report [any of those provided online – preferably Strengths-Based Leadership Report]
>
> Underline or circle items you need more clarification on

The following exercises can be used in presentation settings.

The Strengths Equation

Strength = Talent + Skill + Knowledge

Strength = The ability to consistently provide near-perfect performance in a specific task.

A TRACK EXAMPLE

Strength

A track sprinter's ability to get into and out of the starter's block quickly and cleanly

Skills

Move into the correct "on your mark" position and stance.

Transition into the most efficient "get set" stance.

TALENTS

innate sense of timing, natural relaxation under pressure

Knowledge

From Formal Education (Coaching):

- The best spot for your starting block is determined by the length of your legs.
- Always lead with your dominant, more powerful foot.

From Informal Education (Experience):

- Staying mentally and physically loose "in the blocks" is important and difficult.
- Attention to minute details can be the winning edge.

TALENTS

inherent ability to focus on only one sound, naturally precise self-control

Talent Versus Strengths

COACH

PERSONAL REPORT

Top 5 Strengths

-
-
-
-
-

Talent

- BEING
- SOUL
- POTENTIAL
- CRUDE OIL
- SEED
- RAW

Strength

- DOING
- ROLE
- PERFORMANCE
- REFINED OIL
- FRUIT/FLOWERS
- MATURE

The Basics of Leadership: Me, Them, It

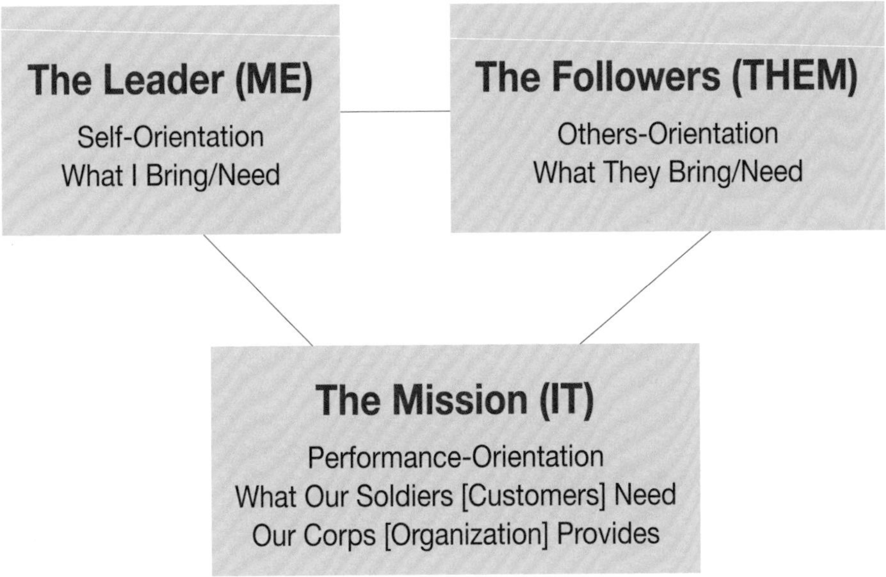

The Leader (ME)
Self-Orientation
What I Bring/Need

The Followers (THEM)
Others-Orientation
What They Bring/Need

The Mission (IT)
Performance-Orientation
What Our Soldiers [Customers] Need
Our Corps [Organization] Provides

Coaching Land Mines . . . When Coaching

- I don't like it!
- I was having a bad day when I took the assessment, so I want to take it again.
- I don't believe it!
- I have too much _____.
- If I take the assessment again, will my results change?
- Are you going to use this information to hire people?

Galatians 5.25-26; 6.4-5 Careful Exploration . . .

WHO YOU ARE

- Your Being
- Understand Your Soul
- I am a Unique Person
- A Satisfied Person

THE WORK YOU HAVE BEEN GIVEN

- Your Doing
- Finding Your Role
- This is My Best Contribution
- A Successful Life

Your Talent Story

Write a three paragraph Talent Story using one of your signature talent themes (example found on pages 67-198):

1. Biographical sketch – focus on you
2. Your talent theme's power and edge – how you utilize it daily
3. Appreciation and application of the biblical narrative or passages associated with you talent them.

For more information or to get involved, visit:

eysjourney.com

Chapter 8

THEME INSIGHT CARDS WITH BALCONIES AND BASEMENTS

Theme Insight Cards have proven to be a favorite among coaches. They are included here for your use. As a bonus, we have provided the content on each theme's Balconies and Basements that coaches can leverage during coaching conversations.

Achiever

People exceptionally talented in the Achiever theme work hard and possess a great deal of stamina. They take immense satisfaction in being busy and productive.

I am (being)	→	a hard worker
I will (doing)	→	set the pace for production
I bring (contribution)	→	intensity and stamina of effort
I need (requirement)	→	freedom to work at my own pace
I love (value)	→	completing tasks
I hate (value)	→	a lack of diligence
Metaphor/Image	→	completing a race, getting to the finish line
Barrier Label	→	work is more important than people

Theme Contrast:

Achiever:	I want to get it done.
Activator:	I want to get it started.

Achiever:	Intense diligence
Intellection:	Intense thinking

Balcony: tireless, strong work ethic, leads by example, go-getter, hungry

Basement: unbalanced, brown-noser, overcommitted, can't say no, burning the candle at both ends, too concentrated on work

Activator

People exceptionally talented in the Activator theme can make things happen by turning thoughts into action. They are often impatient.

I am (being)	→	impatient with inactivity
I will (doing)	→	create momentum
I bring (contribution)	→	a catalytic sense of urgency
I need (requirement)	→	less discussion, more action
I love (value)	→	initiation, instigation
I hate (value)	→	waiting, wasting time
Metaphor/Image	→	getting out of the blocks quickly
Barrier Label	→	leaps before looking

Theme Contrast:

Activator:	There is no substitute for action.
Intellection:	There is no substitute for thinking.

Activator:	Do it until you get it right.
Deliberative:	Do it when you get it right.

Balcony: self-starter, fire-starter, energy source, fearless

Basement: ready-fire-aim, loose cannon, speak before you think, in left field (because others haven't caught up)

Adaptability

People exceptionally talented in the Adaptability theme prefer to go with the flow. They tend to be "now" people who take things as they come and discover the future one day at a time.

I am (being)	→	a here-and-now person
I will (doing)	→	react with immediacy to the immediate
I bring (contribution)	→	a willingness to follow the lead of change
I need (requirement)	→	present pressures that demand an immediate response
I love (value)	→	spontaneity
I hate (value)	→	predictability
Metaphor/Image	→	like a river, go with the flow
Barrier Label	→	directionless

Theme Contrast:

Adaptability:	I like it when every day is different.
Discipline:	I like it when every day is the same.

Adaptability:	Responds to changes in an environment.
Arranger:	Initiates or manages changes in an environment.

Balcony: flexible, comfortable in times of change, easy to get along with, go with the flow

Basement: directionless, indecisive, sheep, inconclusive, whimsical

Analytical

People exceptionally talented in the Analytical theme search for reasons and causes. They have the ability to think about all the factors that might affect a situation.

I am (being)	→	logical and objective in approach
I will (doing)	→	find simplicity in the midst of complexity
I bring (contribution)	→	dispassionate thinking to emotional issues
I need (requirement)	→	time to think
I love (value)	→	data and facts
I hate (value)	→	things that are not or cannot be proven
Metaphor/Image	→	a reduction — boiling down to essence
Barrier Label	→	paralysis by analysis

Theme Contrast:

Analytical:	My head guides me.
Empathy:	My heart guides me.

Analytical:	Truth is objective and must be measured.
Connectedness:	Truth is spiritual and may be invisible.

Balcony: well thought out, logical, deep, thorough, comfortable with numbers, figures, and charts, smart

Basement: rude, short, tough, never-satisfied with the answer, too many questions

Arranger

People exceptionally talented in the Arranger theme can organize, but they also have a flexibility that complements this ability. They like to determine how all of the pieces and resources can be arranged for maximum productivity.

I am (being)	→	comfortable with lots of moving parts
I will (doing)	→	work effectively and efficiently through others
I bring (contribution)	→	flexibility and interactivity
I need (requirement)	→	a dynamic environment
I love (value)	→	initiating and managing necessary change
I hate (value)	→	resistance to necessary change
Metaphor/Image	→	a maestro, a coordinator
Barrier Label	→	difficult to follow because of frequent rearrangements

Theme Contrast:

Arranger:	Multiplicity
Focus:	Singularity

Arranger:	A juggler who momentarily touches all the balls.
Responsibility:	A football player who tenaciously holds on to the ball.

Balcony: flexible, organizer, juggler, aligning and realigning tasks to find the most productive configuration possible, efficient, conductor

Basement: lack of structure, too flexible, don't follow the existing rules or procedures, constantly changing priorities, lack of vision

Belief

People exceptionally talented in the Belief theme have certain core values that are unchanging. Out of these values emerges a defined purpose for their lives.

I am (being)	→	passionate, uncompromising about core values
I will (doing)	→	make sacrifices for things that are important
I bring (contribution)	→	values, stability, clarity, conviction
I need (requirement)	→	a cause or purpose for which to live
I love (value)	→	altruism
I hate (value)	→	anything that does not mesh/align with my beliefs
Metaphor/Image	→	missionary for some idea
Barrier Label	→	set in ways

Theme Contrast:

Belief:	There is only one right way, so I will not be distracted by other paths.
Strategic:	There are many possible ways, so I must consider them all.

Belief:	Seeing comes with believing.
Analytical:	Believing comes with seeing.

Balcony: passionate, steadfast, know where they stand, altruistic, family-oriented, ethical, responsible

Basement: stubborn, set in their ways, elitist, unaccepting of other ideas, opinionated, goody-two-shoes

Command

People exceptionally talented in the Command theme have presence. They can take control of a situation and make decisions.

I am (being)	→	direct and decisive
I will (doing)	→	push back when pushed
I bring (contribution)	→	emotional clarity
I need (requirement)	→	challenges and conflicts
I love (value)	→	exerting control in situations that seem out of control
I hate (value)	→	passivity and avoidance
Metaphor/Image	→	comfortable in the driver's seat
Barrier Label	→	bossy, dictator

Theme Contrast:

Command:	Creates clarity through polarization.
Harmony:	Creates consensus through harmonization.

Command:	People are drawn to you because they know what you think.
Empathy:	People are drawn to you because you know what they feel.

Balcony: charisma, direct, driven, inspirational, easy to follow, clear, concise

Basement: bossy, know-it-all, domineering, rude, abrupt, short, strong-willed, inflexible, stubborn

Communication

People exceptionally talented in the Communication theme generally find it easy to put their thoughts into words. They are good conversationalists and presenters.

I am (being)	→	verbally expressive
I will (doing)	→	connect with others through words
I bring (contribution)	→	attention to messages that must be heard
I need (requirement)	→	a sounding board, an audience
I love (value)	→	stories and storytellers
I hate (value)	→	experience without expression
Metaphor/Image	→	silence is not golden
Barrier Label	→	blabbermouth

Theme Contrast:

Communication:	I think and learn best when I can talk with others.
Intellection:	I think and learn best when I can be alone and quiet.

Communication:	Telling a story helps others understand my message.
Context:	The re-telling of history helps others remember the past.

Balcony: storyteller, great presence, easy to talk to, energizer, entertaining, charismatice

Basement: blabbermouth, poor listener, self-absorbed, show-off, always needs attention

Competition

People exceptionally talented in the Competition theme measure their progress against the performance of others. They strive to win first place and revel in contests.

I am (being)	→	aware of my competitors
I will (doing)	→	strive to win
I bring (contribution)	→	an aspiration to be the best
I need (requirement)	→	peers for comparison and motivation
I love (value)	→	a chance to go against the best
I hate (value)	→	coming in second
Metaphor/Image	→	no consolation prizes — the gold medal is the only medal
Barrier Label	→	sore loser

Theme Contrast:

Competition:	When I watch others perform, I get better.
Significance:	When others watch me perform, I get better.

Competition:	The scoreboard measures my progress and validates victory.
Analytical:	Data quantify experience and validate theories.

Balcony: driven, motivated, number one, measurement-oriented, winner

Basement: sore loser, not a team player, puts down others, self-centered, confrontational

Connectedness

People exceptionally talented in the Connectedness theme have faith in the links among all things. They believe there are few coincidences and that almost every event has meaning.

I am (being)	→	incredibly aware of the borderless and timeless human family
I will (doing)	→	integrate parts into wholes
I bring (contribution)	→	an appreciation of the mystery and wonder of life and all creation
I need (requirement)	→	to be part of something bigger than myself: a family, a team, an organization, a global community, a cosmos
I love (value)	→	circles of life and threads of continuity
I hate (value)	→	an "us vs. them" mentality
Metaphor/Image	→	person as body, mind, and spirit
Barrier Label	→	flaky, new-ager, not in touch with reality

Theme Contrast:

Connectedness:	Accepts mystery.
Analytical:	Proves truth.

Connectedness:	Aware of the inherent, invisible unity that already exists.
Includer:	Aware of the invisible social exclusion that often exists.

Balcony: spiritual, "doesn't sweat the small stuff," strong faith, always looking at the big picture, helps others see purpose

Basement: passive, naïve, too idealistic, wishy-washy

Consistency

People exceptionally talented in the Consistency theme are keenly aware of the need to treat people the same. They try to treat everyone with equality by setting up clear rules and adhering to them.

I am (being)	→	more interested in group needs than individual wants
I will (doing)	→	reduce variance and increase uniformity
I bring (contribution)	→	rules and policies that promote cultural predictability
I need (requirement)	→	standard operating procedures
I love (value)	→	repeating things in the exact same way
I hate (value)	→	unnecessary customization
Metaphor/Image	→	the beauty and efficiency of a consistent golf swing
Barrier Label	→	rules trump relationships and results

Theme Contrast:

Consistency:	Treating people similarly promotes fairness.
Individualization:	Treating people differently promotes fairness.

Consistency:	I like merry-go-rounds.
Adaptability:	I like roller coasters.

Balcony: just, problem-solver, policy-maker

Basement: "by the book," inflexible, unwilling to customize/individualize

Context

People exceptionally talented in the Context theme enjoy thinking about the past. They understand the present by researching its history.

I am (being)	→	appreciative of my predecessors and prior events
I will (doing)	→	remember important history
I bring (contribution)	→	accurate memories and valuable memorabilia
I need (requirement)	→	relevant background for discussions/decisions
I love (value)	→	the retrospective
I hate (value)	→	when the past is forgotten
Metaphor/Image	→	rearview mirror — essential for safe driving
Barrier Label	→	stuck in the past

Theme Contrast:

Context:	I naturally remember and revere what has been.
Futuristic:	I naturally anticipate and imagine what could or should be.

Context:	I can proceed when I understand the history.
Focus:	I can proceed when the goal is clear.

Balcony: has a robust historical frame of reference, learns lessons from the past, knows how things came to be, can leverage knowledge of the past

Basement: slow to move and react to change, closed-minded, lives in the past

Deliberative

People exceptionally talented in the Deliberative theme are best described by the serious care they take in making decisions or choices. They anticipate obstacles.

I am (being)	→	a vigilant observer of potential risk
I will (doing)	→	anticipate things that could go wrong
I bring (contribution)	→	a thorough and conscientious approach
I need (requirement)	→	time to listen and think before being expected to speak
I love (value)	→	restraint and caution in the face of risk
I hate (value)	→	a rush to judgment
Metaphor/Image	→	an ounce of prevention is worth a pound of cure; a jury must deliberate before there is a verdict
Barrier Label	→	hesitant — it's the early bird that gets the worm

Theme Contrast:

Deliberative:	Like a brake, I tend to slow things down.
Activator:	Like an accelerator, I tend to speed things up.

Deliberative:	Socially cautious
Woo:	Socially adventurous

Balcony: good judgment, identifies risk, makes solid decisions, can plan for the unexpected

Basement: standoffish, aloof, cautious, slow, introverted, afraid to act

Developer

People exceptionally talented in the Developer theme recognize and cultivate the potential in others. They spot the signs of each small improvement and derive satisfaction from evidence of progress.

I am (being)	→	patient with the inexperienced and unseasoned
I will (doing)	→	get satisfaction from the growth of others
I bring (contribution)	→	a commitment (time and energy) to human growth
I need (requirement)	→	someone to invest in
I love (value)	→	human potential and progress
I hate (value)	→	wasted or unrealized potential
Metaphor/Image	→	a parent's patience with a baby learning to walk
Barrier Label	→	wastes time on low performers

Theme Contrast:

Developer:	I notice and promote growth in others.
Maximizer:	I notice and promote excellence.

Developer:	Interested in getting people done.
Achiever:	Interested in getting work done.

Balcony: grows talent in others, teacher, coach, enjoys helping others succeed, invests in others

Basement: not an individual contributor, wastes time on low-potential people, spectator

Discipline

People exceptionally talented in the Discipline theme enjoy routine and structure. Their world is best described by the order they create.

I am (being)	→	an efficient manager of limited resources
I will (doing)	→	plan in advance and then follow the plan
I bring (contribution)	→	precision and detail orientation
I need (requirement)	→	a structured and organized environment
I love (value)	→	things that are organized and orderly
I hate (value)	→	chaos and confusion, flying by the seat of one's pants
Metaphor/Image	→	having their ducks in a row
Barrier Label	→	may be resistant to change

Theme Contrast:

Discipline:	I meet deadlines because it makes me feel good.
Responsibility:	I meet deadlines because it makes others respect me.

Discipline:	Can't see the forest for the trees.
Connectedness:	Can't see the trees for the forest.

Balcony: high productivity and accuracy because of ability to structure, breaks down complex into steps, great planners, promotes efficiency

Basement: overbearing, rigid, mechanized, can't handle change

Empathy

People exceptionally talented in the Empathy theme can sense other people's feelings by imagining themselves in others' lives or situations.

I am (being)	→	an emotional person
I will (doing)	→	make the visceral explicit
I bring (contribution)	→	emotional intelligence
I need (requirement)	→	freedom to laugh, cry, vent
I love (value)	→	the gladness, sadness, madness of humanity
I hate (value)	→	those things that block or limit emotional expression
Metaphor/Image	→	a person's affect will often determine his or her effect
Barrier Label	→	bleeding heart

Theme Contrast:

Empathy:	I usually can tell how someone feels.
Individualization:	I usually can tell who someone is.

Empathy:	Intuition helps me decide what to do.
Analytical:	Data helps me decide what to do.

Balcony: creates trust, brings healing, knows just what to say/do, customizes approach to others

Basement: "soft," moody, over-involved

Focus

People exceptionally talented in the Focus theme can take a direction, follow through, and make the corrections necessary to stay on track. They prioritize, then act.

I am (being)	→	intensely and intentionally single-minded
I will (doing)	→	persevere until the goal is reached
I bring (contribution)	→	clarity through concentration and direction
I need (requirement)	→	a goal to establish priorities
I love (value)	→	to begin with the end in mind
I hate (value)	→	going off on misdirected tangents
Metaphor/Image	→	"in the zone"
Barrier Label	→	destination mentality may limit enjoyment of the journey

Theme Contrast:

Focus:	I have a goal.
Futuristic:	I have a dream.

Focus:	I have a goal I plan to reach.
Discipline:	I have a plan to reach my goal.

Balcony: point person, disciplined, purposeful, laser-like precision, identifies important areas quickly, goal-setter and goal-getter

Basement: absorbed, tough to relax, intense, stressed

Futuristic

People exceptionally talented in the Futuristic theme are inspired by the future and what could be. They energize others with their visions of the future.

I am (being)	→	fascinated with tomorrow
I will (doing)	→	anticipate and imagine what could or should be
I bring (contribution)	→	previews, predictions, forecasts
I need (requirement)	→	opportunities to talk about the foreseen future
I love (value)	→	the inspiration that comes from dreaming
I hate (value)	→	contentment with the status quo
Metaphor/Image	→	visionary
Barrier Label	→	head in the clouds

Theme Contrast:

Futuristic:	I'm so preoccupied with tomorrow that I'm not ready for today.
Adaptability:	I'm so occupied with today that I'm not ready for tomorrow.

Futuristic:	I can see a better world.
Strategic:	I can see the route that will take us to a better world.

Balcony: imaginative, creative, visionary, even prophetic, inspiring

Basement: dreamer, "Fantasy Island," out in left field, lacks pragmatism

Harmony

People exceptionally talented in the Harmony theme look for consensus. They don't enjoy conflict; rather, they seek areas of agreement.

I am (being)	→	calm, even-keeled
I will (doing)	→	seek to eliminate the waste of emotional energy
I bring (contribution)	→	a peace-loving, conflict-resistant approach
I need (requirement)	→	areas of agreement, common ground
I love (value)	→	the sacrifice of personal agendas to facilitate group performance
I hate (value)	→	negative effects of friction
Metaphor/Image	→	smoothing ruffled feathers
Barrier Label	→	afraid of conflict

Theme Contrast:

Harmony:	Let's do what works best.
Belief:	I want to do what matters most.

Harmony:	Being interdependent, I willingly defer to experts.
Self-Assurance:	Being independent, I confidently rely on my own expertise.

Balcony: negotiator, can see both sides of a situation, great at asking questions, able to arrive at consensus, great facilitator

Basement: weak, indecisive, non-confrontational, avoids conflict

Ideation

People exceptionally talented in the Ideation theme are fascinated by ideas. They are able to find connections between seemingly disparate phenomena.

I am (being)	→	unaffected by the ambiguity and risk of innovation
I will (doing)	→	think outside the box
I bring (contribution)	→	new and fresh perspectives
I need (requirement)	→	freedom to explore possibilities without restraints or limits
I love (value)	→	coming up with something brand new
I hate (value)	→	doing what we have always done
Metaphor/Image	→	creativity of an artist, blank canvas or page, lump of clay
Barrier Label	→	impractical

Theme Contrast:

Ideation:	I open the windows of my mind to increase the possibility of discovery.
Focus:	I close the windows of my mind to decrease the possibility of distraction.

Ideation:	A blue-sky approach of creative innovation is the best way to get a competitive advantage.
Harmony:	The down-to-earth approach of efficient collaboration is the best way to get a competitive advantage.

Balcony: invites others in, caring, engages others, sensitive, takes up for others

Basement: indiscriminate, unable to decide, generous to a fault

Includer

People exceptionally talented in the Includer theme accept others. They show awareness of those who feel left out and make an effort to include them.

I am (being)	→	aware of exclusion and understand its repercussions
I will (doing)	→	shrink the gap between the haves and have-nots
I bring (contribution)	→	a high-level of tolerance and acceptance of diversity
I need (requirement)	→	room for everyone
I love (value)	→	assimilation and integration
I hate (value)	→	cliques
Metaphor/Image	→	cliques are breeding grounds for clichéd thinking
Barrier Label	→	indiscriminate

Theme Contrast:

Includer:	I work for the acceptance of those on the outside.
Harmony:	I work for the agreement of those on the inside.

Includer:	Be indiscriminately accepting of all who are on the bus.
Maximizer:	Be discriminatingly selective about who gets on the bus.

Balcony: invites others in, caring, engages others, sensitive, takes up for others

Basement: indiscriminate, unable to decide, generous to a fault

Individualization

People exceptionally talented in the Individualization theme are intrigued with the unique qualities of each person. They have a gift for figuring out how people who are different can work together productively.

I am (being)	→	a customizer
I will (doing)	→	see the potential in human diversity rather than its problem
I bring (contribution)	→	an understanding of people that is valuable for placement
I need (requirement)	→	individual expectations that are created to fit a person
I love (value)	→	people getting to do what they do best
I hate (value)	→	a one-size-fits-all approach
Metaphor/Image	→	casting director — uses intelligence about people
Barrier Label	→	sacrifices group need for individual needs

Theme Contrast:

Individualization:	I know who you are.
Relator:	I want to know you, and I want you to know me.

Individualization:	Starts with a person and finds the right job for him.
Arranger:	Starts with a job that needs to get done and finds the right person for it.

Balcony: sees the uniqueness in all individuals, intuitively knows that "one size doesn't fit all," appreciates the differences in others

Basement: unable to synthesize when it comes to people, has difficulty placing group above individual, difficulty in making people decisions

Input

People exceptionally talented in the Input theme have a craving to know more. Often they like to collect and archive all kinds of information.

I am (being)	→	utilitarian resource collector
I will (doing)	→	hang on to things that could be helpful resources for others
I bring (contribution)	→	tangible tools that can facilitate growth and performance
I need (requirement)	→	space to store the resources I naturally acquire
I love (value)	→	to provide relevant and tangible help
I hate (value)	→	not having things that would be useful to others
Metaphor/Image	→	sponge — absorbent (input) dispenser (output)
Barrier Label	→	packrat with too much lying around

Theme Contrast:

Input:	I love to collect things that are potentially helpful.
Learner:	I love the process of learning.

Input:	I help people by sharing tangible tools I have acquired.
Ideation:	I help people by sharing creative ideas I have conceived.

Balcony: great resource, knowledgeable, excellent memory, mind for detail, collects interesting things, excellent conversationalist

Basement: knows a lot of worthless information, packrat, cluttered house-cluttered mind, boring conversationalist

Intellection

People exceptionally talented in the Intellection theme are characterized by their intellectual activity. They are introspective and appreciate intellectual discussions.

I am (being)	→	conceptual, deep, solitary
I will (doing)	→	see thinking as synonymous with doing
I bring (contribution)	→	depth of understanding and wisdom
I need (requirement)	→	time for reflection and meditation
I love (value)	→	the theoretical because it is the precursor to the practical
I hate (value)	→	a thoughtless approach to anything
Metaphor/Image	→	drilling deep, plumbing the depths
Barrier Label	→	isolated and aloof

Theme Contrast:

Intellection:	An inquiring approach to growth and learning.
Input:	An acquiring approach to growth and learning.

Intellection:	Thinks about concepts that need to be understood.
Restorative:	Thinks about problems that need to be solved.

Balcony: excellent thinker, enjoys musing, capable of deep and philosophical thought, able to work alone

Basement: a loner, slow to act or wastes time thinking too much, isolated, doesn't work well with others

Learner

People exceptionally talented in the Learner theme have a great desire to learn and want to continuously improve. The process of learning, rather than the outcome, excites them.

I am (being)	→	one who enjoys the experience of being a learner
I will (doing)	→	follow the things that interest me
I bring (contribution)	→	a learning perspective
I need (requirement)	→	exposure to new information and experiences
I love (value)	→	to live on the frontier/the cutting edge
I hate (value)	→	knowing it all and know-it-alls
Metaphor/Image	→	yes to learning curves, no to learning plateaus
Barrier Label	→	curiosity may lead to irrelevance or non-productivity

Theme Contrast:

Learner:	My interests guide my intentions.
Focus:	My intentions guide my interests.

Learner:	I am always interested in learning something new.
Woo:	I am always interested in meeting someone new.

Balcony: always learning, catches on quickly, interested in many things, finds life intriguing

Basement: a know it all, lacks focus on results, learns a lot – produces little, bookish

Maximizer

People exceptionally talented in the Maximizer theme focus on strengths as a way to stimulate personal and group excellence. They seek to transform something strong into something superb.

I am (being)	→	committed to excellence
I will (doing)	→	focus on what is strong and manage around what is weak
I bring (contribution)	→	a quality orientation
I need (requirement)	→	quality to be valued as much as quantity
I love (value)	→	a maximum return on investments
I hate (value)	→	an obsession with weakness fixing
Metaphor/Image	→	good-to-great, good-better-best
Barrier Label	→	picky, never satisfied

Theme Contrast:

Maximizer:	I aspire to meet or exceed a standard of excellence.
Competition:	I aspire to be number one.

Maximizer:	I want to build something great.
Restorative:	I want to fix something broken.

Balcony: mastery, success, excellence, working with the best

Basement: perfectionist, picky, never good enough, always reworking

Positivity

People exceptionally talented in the Positivity theme have contagious enthusiasm. They are upbeat and can get others excited about what they are going to do.

I am (being)	→	optimistic, hopeful, fun-loving
I will (doing)	→	lift and lighten emotional environments
I bring (contribution)	→	contagious energy and enthusiasm
I need (requirement)	→	freedom to experience the joy and drama of life
I love (value)	→	living life to its fullest
I hate (value)	→	negative people who drain the life out of others
Metaphor/Image	→	glass is half full, not half empty
Barrier Label	→	naïve

Theme Contrast:

Positivity:	light-hearted
Analytical:	serious-minded

Positivity:	Praise can't be overdone, so I am generous with it.
Deliberative:	Praise can be overdone, so I use it sparingly.

Balcony: enthusiastic, lighthearted, energetic, generous with praise, optimistic

Basement: insincere, naïve, superficial, Pollyanna

Relator

People exceptionally talented in the Relator theme enjoy close relationships with others. They find deep satisfaction in working hard with friends to achieve a goal.

I am (being)	→	genuine and authentic
I will (doing)	→	get to know more about the people closest to me
I bring (contribution)	→	social depth and transparency
I need (requirement)	→	time and opportunities for one-on-one interactions
I love (value)	→	close, caring, mutual relationships
I hate (value)	→	the initial social discomfort of meeting someone new
Metaphor/Image	→	knowing and being known by friends
Barrier Label	→	cliquish cronyism

Theme Contrast:

Relator:	Socially transparent, I invite my friends in.
Includer:	Socially inclusive, I invite outsiders in.

Relator:	I want to get to know more about the people I already know.
Woo:	I want to get to know more people.

Balcony: caring, trusting, a great friend, forgiving, generous

Basement: lives in a clique, crony, has an inner circle, plays favorites

Responsibility

People exceptionally talented in the Responsibility theme take psychological ownership of what they say they will do. They are committed to stable values such as honesty and loyalty.

I am (being)	→	someone others often trust to get things done
I will (doing)	→	keep promises and follow through on commitments
I bring (contribution)	→	dependability and loyalty
I need (requirement)	→	freedom to take ownership
I love (value)	→	the respect of others
I hate (value)	→	disappointing others and being disappointed by others
Metaphor/Image	→	serious owner — not disinterested renter
Barrier Label	→	can't say no or let go

Theme Contrast:

Responsibility:	If you can't do it right, don't do it.
Activator:	Doing something is always better than not doing anything.

Responsibility:	I feel intense guilt when I fail to do something right.
Significance:	I feel intense regret when I miss an opportunity to succeed.

Balcony: committed, accountable, independent, trusted, conscientious

Basement: micro-manager, obsessive, can't say "no," takes on too much

Restorative

People exceptionally talented in the Restorative theme are adept at dealing with problems. They are good at figuring out what is wrong and resolving it.

I am (being)	→	not intimidated by points of pain or dysfunction
I will (doing)	→	look for the bug in the system, diagnose what ails
I bring (contribution)	→	courage and creativity to problematic situations
I need (requirement)	→	problems that must be solved
I love (value)	→	finding solutions
I hate (value)	→	the idea that problems will disappear if they are ignored
Metaphor/Image	→	medical model
Barrier Label	→	perceived as negative because of association with problems

Theme Contrast:

Restorative:	Trouble-shooter
Strategic:	Map-maker

Restorative:	I intentionally invade problem areas to restore the original state.
Positivity:	I intentionally evade problem areas to maintain my emotional state.

Balcony: problem solver, troubleshooter, finds improvements and solutions

Basement: focuses on weaknesses, punitive, negative, critical

Self-Assurance

People exceptionally talented in the Self-Assurance theme feel confident in their ability to manage their own lives. They possess an inner compass that gives them confidence that their decisions are right.

I am (being)	→	internally confident in the midst of external uncertainty
I will (doing)	→	seek to exert influence rather than be influenced
I bring (contribution)	→	a willingness to take necessary risks
I need (requirement)	→	freedom to act unilaterally and independently
I love (value)	→	being in control of my own destiny
I hate (value)	→	others telling me what to do
Metaphor/Image	→	internal compass, marches to beat of different drum
Barrier Label	→	arrogant, over-confident, self-sufficient

Theme Contrast:

Self-Assurance:	Anticipates risk so that it can be engaged and overcome.
Deliberative:	Anticipates risk so that it can be avoided and minimized.

Self-Assurance:	Certainty
Learner:	Curiosity

Balcony: self-confident, strong inner compass, risk-taker

Basement: arrogant, self-righteous, over confident, stubborn

Significance

People exceptionally talented in the Significance theme want to be very important in the eyes of others. They are independent and want to be recognized.

I am (being)	→	interested in being seen as significant so that I can accomplish something significant
I will (doing)	→	be motivated and influenced by the perceptions of others
I bring (contribution)	→	a desire for wanting more
I need (requirement)	→	an appreciative audience that will bring out my best
I love (value)	→	associating with successful people
I hate (value)	→	being invisible or ignored by others
Metaphor/Image	→	natural performer who is comfortable with the visibility of center stage/bright lights
Barrier Label	→	attention hound, showboat

Theme Contrast:

Significance:	I want to be admired so I must do something admirable.
Woo:	I want to win others over so I must be winsome.

Significance:	To be seen and heard is my desire.
Deliberative:	To watch and listen is my desire.

Balcony: seeks outstanding performance, does things of importance, independent

Basement: recognition hungry, self-focused, needy

Strategic

People exceptionally talented in the Strategic theme create alternative ways to proceed. Faced with any given scenario, they can quickly spot the relevant patterns and issues.

I am (being)	→	willing to consider all the possibilities so the best isn't missed
I will (doing)	→	find the best route moving forward
I bring (contribution)	→	creative anticipation, imagination, persistence
I need (requirement)	→	freedom to make mid-course corrections
I love (value)	→	seeing a way when others assume there is no way
I hate (value)	→	doing things the way we have always done them
Metaphor/Image	→	great peripheral vision — can see the whole field
Barrier Label	→	always has to try something different

Theme Contrast:

Strategic:	Natural evaluator of possibilities.
Analytical:	Natural evaluator of realities.

Strategic:	Considers alternative routes.
Focus:	Concentrates on a singular destination.

Balcony: anticipates alternatives, intuitive, sees different paths

Basement: jumps to quick decisions, difficult to understand their thinking, closed-minded

Woo

People exceptionally talented in the Woo theme love the challenge of meeting new people and winning them over. They derive satisfaction from breaking the ice and making a connection with someone.

I am (being)	→	socially fast and outgoing
I will (doing)	→	take the social initiative
I bring (contribution)	→	energy to social situations
I need (requirement)	→	social variability
I love (value)	→	meeting someone I haven't met before
I hate (value)	→	a static or shrinking social network
Metaphor/Image	→	hand-shaking politician, building his constituency
Barrier Label	→	phony, superficial

Theme Contrast:

Woo:	Can build a broad social network.
Relator:	Can build a deep social network.

Woo:	Winning others over.
Competition:	Winning over others.

Balcony: outgoing, people-oriented, networker, rapport-builder

Basement: fake, shallow, does not care about deep relationships

ACKNOWLEDGMENTS

There are so many individuals who helped make this book a reality, and we are grateful to them all.

We express sincere and heartfelt gratitude to the U.S. Military Chaplains, Chaplain Assistants, and religious support teams that faithfully helped us develop and implement the *Engage Your Strengths* program.

Many thanks to James Puchy, American Bible Society's Chief Redevelopment Officer. His desire to see *Engage Your Strengths* program expand and influence millions, encouraged us to dream bigger.

Thank you to Jeremy Pietrocini and Scott Brown for their leadership of Gallup's Faith Practice over the past five years. Their support and encouragement kept this project alive.

We express sincere gratitude to our EYS Champions and Coaches who not only have lived their strengths, but who have helped thousands to do the same. Their stories have made this edition a testimony to our Creator!

Special thanks to our Project Manager, Chaplain (Captain) Dave Keller, U.S. Army Reserves. He was a driving force behind EYS 3.0 and his Achiever went into hyper-drive to make this edition a reality. Thank you to our Project Designer, Caleb Komorowski. Without his creative genius, this project would not be what it is today. A special thanks to Stacey Wright for the extraordinary editing that made this book possible. Thank you to Becky Puchy who has journeyed with us from the beginning and to a host of other ABS associates who made significant contributions to the *Engage Your Strengths* project, including Donna Fitzgerald, and John Greco. Thanks to the Gallup® Team made up of Alana Draus, Todd Jensen, and Mark Bartels.

AUTHORS

Dr. John Edgar Caterson

Strategic | Activator | Futuristic | Achiever | Self-Assurance

John Edgar Caterson is a GALLUP® Certified Strengths Coach and the cultural architect of the *Engage Your Strengths* Program. He is the founder, president, and CEO of American Strengths Center.

John Edgar attended Toccoa Falls College, Princeton Theological Seminary, The University of Edinburgh in Scotland, and The Beeson International Center at Asbury Theological Seminary. He holds an undergraduate degree in Philosophy and Religion, a Masters degree in Divinity, was a Supervised Post-Graduate Fellow, and holds a Doctorate in four disciplines – Story Integration, Narrative Theology, Leadership, and Psychology. He has co-authored two children's books – *Acts Tracks* and *Bible Trek: Luke*. John Edgar was born in Philadelphia. He lives with his bride Kristi, son Gabriel Isaiah, and two daughters Annabelle Grace and Aliza Hope, near Tampa Bay in Lithia, Florida.

John Edgar likes to start each day by asking the question, "What about the roof?" [an alternate route]. The story of the "Four Strategic Friends" in Mark 2 has been a major influence on his life. "*Because of the crowd, however, they [the four friends] could not get the man to him. So they made a hole in the roof right above the place where Jesus was.*" These friends would not be denied. Faced with an obstacle they stepped back, gathered their thoughts, and went to the roof . . . Jesus' response was proof that their actions were noticed . . .

Rev. Curt Liesveld

Responsibility | Relator | Maximizer | Learner | Analytical

Curt Liesveld was a practitioner, author, and Senior Learning and Development Consultant with the Gallup® Organization. He joined Gallup® in 1999, and became one of Gallup®'s leading authorities on the Clifton StrengthsFinder® and its corresponding strengths-based approach to human development. He led hundreds of strengths-based development programs for leaders, managers and coaches, provided strengths coaching for thousands of individuals and wrote extensively about the CSF tool and its use for personal, professional and organizational development. Liesveld was a co-author of *Living Your Strengths*, a Gallup® publication that applies Gallup®'s tools and science to faith-based communities and settings. An experienced Strengths Practitioner, he played a significant role in the development and global delivery of Gallup®'s suite of Strengths Coach Development programs. Prior to his career at Gallup®, Liesveld spent 23 years as a church leader and pastor.

Curt was born in Holland, Nebraska. He earned a Bachelors of Arts in Sociology from the University of Nebraska, a Masters of Arts in Counseling Psychology from the University of Nebraska, and a Masters of Divinity in Theology from Western Theological Seminary in Holland, Michigan.

Some of Curt's most impactful quotes are: "Getting clarity about the unique nature of my soul can help me find my best way to fulfill my chosen roles and to meet my chosen goals." "The greatest temptation a person will face is the temptation to live someone else's life." "I like to start with their CSF themes and move to their life." "There is something broken in each of us that we cannot fix. There is something powerful in each of us that we must not waste."

Chaplain (Colonel) Art Pace (U.S. Army, Retired)

Positivity | Woo | Communication | Connectedness | Individualization

Arthur "Art" Pace is a Gallup Strength Performance Coach. He pastored a church for three years before entering the U.S. Army as a chaplain in 1982. Achieving the rank of Colonel, he retired in 2012 after 30 years of service. He then went on to serve in various capacities with American Bible Society, Wycliffe Associates, The 1687 Foundation, Olive Branch International, and Planting Roots.

Art was born in Camden, New Jersey. He earned a Bachelor of Science degree in Environmental Science from Rutgers University, a Masters of Divinity degree from Gordon-Conwell Theological Seminary, and a Masters of Strategic Studies degree from the United States Army War College. He has been married to the former Mary Modzelewski since 1975. They have two grown and married children, Megan and Theresa, who are still the joy of their lives. He is also the proud grandfather of Sydney and Juliet Dickerson.

When Art was a child, his father once asked him if he knew the two things that all people have in common. When Art did not know, his father said, "All people have two things in common: they have a story to tell, and are looking for someone they can tell their story to. When you grow up son, try to be the one that they want to tell their stories to." Art still seeks to be the one to who people are willing to tell their stories.

We need your help. How has this book impacted your life?

Dear Armed Services Member,

American Bible Society is honored to share God's Word with brave heroes like you who have faithfully served or are currently serving our country.

Generous contributions from our supporters make it possible for us to provide these resources to you free of charge. As a way of thanking these faithful supporters, we love to share stories of how their contributions have made a difference in someone's life.

Will you take a moment to tell us about your journey? It's easy online at **ASMFeedback.com**, or simply scan the QR code for quick access from your device. You can also mail us your response using the enclosed postage-paid card.

You may provide us with your name, or remain anonymous.

Thank you and God bless you!

Rev. Dr. Paul McCullough
Armed Services Ministry, Senior Manager for Customer Relations
Email: **Provisions@AmericanBible.org**

Check out American Bible Society,
Armed Services Ministry website:
https://armedservicesministry.org